*The winner ain't the one with the fastest car, it's the one that refused to lose.*
— Dale Earnhardt

# BUCKLE UP
## FOR BUSINESS SUCCESS

**YOUR ROAD MAP FOR
THE WILD RIDE
OF SMALL BUSINESS OWNERSHIP**

# LISA REINICKE
CEO OF AUTOMOTIVE WARRANTY NETWORK

*Our House Publications*

Our House Publications
Copyright 2020 by Our House Publications
All rights reserved.

No part of this book may be reproduced in any form—written, electronic, recording or photo-copying—without written permission from the publisher or author. The exception would be in the case of brief quotations embodied in critical articles and reviews and pages where permission is specifically granted by the publisher or author.

Although every precaution has been taken to verify the accuracy of the information contained herein, the author and publisher assume no responsibility for any errors or omissions. No liability is assumed for damages that may result from the use of information contained within.

Names have been changed to protect the privacy of individuals.
Edited by Alexandra O'Connell
Cover and Interior Design by Bublish, Inc.
Distributed by Bublish, Inc.

Library of Congress Control Number: 2019912878
ISBN: 978-0-9997639-0-2 (Trade paperback)
ISBN: 978-0-9997639-1-9 (Ebook)
To order bulk sales for organizations and schools
contact Kayla@LisaReinicke.com
Other books by Lisa Reinicke and Our House Publications:

Football Flyboy
Wilhelmina's Wish
Bart's Escape Out the Gate
Arnold, the Cute Little Pig with Personality
David's Christmas Wish
Wings and Feet

Visit us at www.LisaReinicke.com
Printed in USA

*You can- you will-don't give up and don't stay still.
Remember to laugh and cry along the way
because tomorrow's a new day.
Keep your business passion but don't
lose your human compassion.*

# Contents

Introduction ..................................................................... ix

Chapter 1   The Gift .......................................................... 1
Chapter 2   Out with the Old ........................................... 7
Chapter 3   Victimitis ..................................................... 16
Chapter 4   Court ............................................................ 24
Chapter 5   Work Ethic .................................................. 30
Chapter 6   Automotive Warranty Network is Born ...... 36
Chapter 7   You'll Never Grow Alone ............................ 44
Chapter 8   Whale Tails .................................................. 52
Chapter 9   Business is Business .................................... 58
Chapter 10 Creating a New Department ....................... 69
Chapter 11 Patience and Persistence .............................. 78
Chapter 12 Honesty is the Best Policy .......................... 85
Chapter 13 Adventure ...................................................... 91
Chapter 14 Keep Moving, No Matter What ................. 98
Chapter 15 Intimidation ................................................ 104
Chapter 16 FHB ............................................................. 109

| Chapter 17 | Perspective | 114 |
| Chapter 18 | Desperation | 124 |
| Chapter 19 | Gut and Instinct—You Can't Explain It | 133 |
| Chapter 20 | Midnight Worship | 139 |
| Chapter 21 | Don't Be a Dumbass | 144 |
| Chapter 22 | Healing from Reeling | 152 |
| Chapter 23 | Viewpoint is Everything | 162 |
| Chapter 24 | Embracing Technology | 169 |
| Chapter 25 | Peacock Suits | 177 |
| Chapter 26 | Moses Would Have Had a Computer | 184 |
| Chapter 27 | Dirty Rotten Scoundrels | 191 |
| Chapter 28 | Hatchet Man | 197 |
| Chapter 29 | Geez, Don't Get Defensive | 203 |
| Chapter 30 | Succession—Ugh, I Never Want to Leave | 208 |
| Chapter 31 | The Halfway Point is Not the End | 218 |
| Epilogue | | 223 |

| | | |
|---|---|---|
| Authors Note | | 225 |
| Acknowledgements | | 227 |
| About the Author | | 229 |

# Introduction

Most business books instruct readers on the basic concepts of what you should or shouldn't do to be successful. Real life often throws a monkey wrench into the perfect instructions that you were trying to follow. Furthermore, your views change as you mature. You grow in wisdom about life in general and in the business world of hard knocks.

As you listen to motivational speakers, chances are, there is a small window of excitement driving you to conquer the next aspect of your company goals. The window soon closes as reality slaps you in the face, and the motivation gives way to necessity. Everything the speaker said is quickly put away and the day-to-day problems have you falling back into your same old hole.

There is a cost in owning any size company. The price will either be money or time; it probably will be both. Also, tagging along are risks that need to be taken. Sometimes your first instinct is not the best, but taking no chances at all means you—and your business—become stagnant.

As you navigate daily decisions, start noticing that you begin to pay for items that you need long before you purchase them. The story of our paper feed comes to mind. Our paper feed for the printer was broken and I did not want to pay for a new one out of my limited budget. Every morning, staff stood patiently in front of the printer, pulling out individual pages as they were printed. After months of this, my husband spent my hard-earned money on a new feeder. I was furious; however, the staff now had an extra two hours a day to produce more revenue for the company. I had wasted immeasurable time, which translated into lost money, long before that paper feed was purchased.

This book is full of similar stories that will demonstrate how to make lasting changes in your business. The lessons may alter your point of view as you navigate a growing company. By using my personal examples of successes and failures, you will be able to use your own judgment when you see a problem arise in your company. I use humor a lot because laughter engraves in the memory what we need to retain for later use.

I see many people that have great intentions when starting a business. Whether it is a small endeavor or they want to take over the market, their aspiration can be a reality. Countless entrepreneurs often give up too soon, or don't put in the effort to move the needle forward. If your dream is strong enough, you can achieve *the dream you seek*—and my hope is that these stories can help you get there.

# CHAPTER 1

# The Gift

*"I want to learn how to drive
the doggone thing."*

Woohoo, I love presents! The big ones, the little ones, stupid ones, and extraordinarily expensive ones are all great gifts. Suppose you receive a gift that isn't just any present—but an excellent, glorious, extravagant offering that doesn't cost you a dime.

The item now in your possession is freely offered to you with no strings attached but does have an instruction manual in the language that you can read. There are several warnings throughout the booklet with words of caution: "DANGER! FAILURE TO FOLLOW INSTRUCTIONS MAY LEAD TO UNDESIRED RESULTS."

Instructions are made for stupid people, right? Almost all directions and warnings are dumb. "Don't throw the hair dryer in the bathtub." Who really needs this warning? I, for one, know that I have disregarded warnings and proceeded to use products the way I felt made sense at the time. I most certainly always cut off the "do not remove" tag from all my pillows. The pillow police haven't caught me yet.

Other manuals are important; however, I can end up skipping steps that don't seem necessary, in my opinion. Sometimes, the results turn out pretty good. At other times, I find myself taking apart a "do-it-yourself" kit and starting over. I usually choose to use the instructions the second time around. Luckily, IKEA is patient with all the do-it-yourselfers when they return a product presumably packaged without the needed part.

Now, let's suppose that the most excellent gift you receive is a Bugatti race car—a state-of-the-art one. It's new, never been driven, with the smell of pure leather inside, and has all the latest intelligent technology…much like our human brains. There are a hundred different settings for speed, distance, lane changing, and optimal performance. The racing engine also goes very fast, so the trip doesn't take long at all. Enjoying the adventure will be over before you can blink twice.

On receiving such a unique item, there are several ways we as ordinary human creatures react:

One person might say, "What in the heck am I going to

do with a race car? I can't drive a race car. Heck, I can't even drive the vehicle around town."

Those people never move on to doing anything with the gifted car except to let the vehicle sit in the yard or driveway, cluttering up the place.

> **"I can't do it. So I am not going to try."**

Another person might have visions of fame in his or her head…imagining booze, food, and sitting poolside with beautiful people at their estate drinking in their wealth. Butlers with trays of champagne and bonbons serve guests as musicians entertain their new friends. In other words, sell the car, take the money, and party like there is no tomorrow. Using the funds will at least give this person momentary happiness and joy.

> **"I am only in it for the short run. No commitments."**

Then there are those that would think that having a Bugatti is very cool. These people might let a professional driver learn the ropes, with the stipulation that they catch a ride and enjoy the trip. It's free for the driver to use as long as the owner can tag along on the adventure. The gift is enjoyed by someone else and in this scenario, you become a second fiddle.

> **"Let someone else do it, not me."**

Finally, there are the few who decide, "I want to learn to drive this doggone thing. I am going to be the pilot of my own adventure." These people know that learning to drive will take an immense amount of hard work, self-discipline, and dedication. Even after they learn to operate the vehicle, they are going to need support. Every race driver needs a great co-pilot, pit crew, and an excellent maintenance crew to have a successful trip anywhere. To achieve the ultimate goal will take time and money.

In racing, spotters watch the race track. These are trained professionals who watch the road during a race and lead the driver safely through takeoff, laps, and finish. They are our eyes and ears for the race. We need to listen to them and talk to them frequently.

Every driver should have a pre-race checklist to follow. Most professionals can tell you that they know the items on this list by heart, but they still review each item religiously before they launch onto the speedway. The goal isn't only to get to the next destination as quickly as possible, but to arrive safely and not harm any soul along the way.

Learning to drive the car is where our story will begin; your life is the gift, and it is a one-time offering. Wherever you are in life, realize that one fact right now. If you are *not* choosing to be the pilot of your own craft, don't read this book. The book will be lessons for those determined to put in all the time, money, and effort needed to reach your goal. My Dad would say blood, sweat, and tears are needed as well.

You have a destiny, if you choose to follow it. My destiny wasn't the homes I have lived in; it was the cars. Life was where vehicles took me, and the people who were there sitting in the front and back seats with me. It was the times we enjoyed together getting to our destination, wherever that might have been. From the start, for me, life was all about the car.

My granddaddy owned a dealership, my Dad worked for the manufacturer, and I was destined to grow up a car brat. Using the automobile as inspiration, you can substitute your own passion in the examples I use throughout the story.

Learning to drive a Bugatti isn't easy, and it's a lengthy task. It is often expensive and could take patience along the way. So, "Buckle Up, Buckwheat"—let's check out the new vehicle and see the equipment on board!

**Lesson Learned:** Your life is the gift—drive it to your destiny, make the most of every corner, watch the weather conditions, and evaluate your route. Listen to your spotters along the way.

A complete stock of genuine factory replacement parts which enables us to give a factory approved service job on De Soto and Plymouth automobiles.

We have new De Soto and Plymouth motors in stock and can give immediate installation service.

Bring us your automobile for a free appraisal and estimate of the cost of making necessary repairs or installing a new motor.

We have no new cars to offer you, but we do give our personal attention and service on all repair jobs which makes many satisfied customers because of this individual service.

JOHN COOK

# PERKINS & COOK MOTOR CO.
## De SOTO – PLYMOUTH

JOHN COOK     BILL PERKINS

121 North Beard     Shawnee, Oklahoma     Phone 468

The dealership my grandfather owned

# CHAPTER 2

# Out with the Old

*"Shell-shock. How did it get this far away from me?"*

"The police are here. Did you get them? We only have a few seconds. We won't be able to get anything else after we leave. So get whatever you can now. There is no coming back." Rich hurried me down the aisle of the office, surrounded by cubicles with employees who were desperate to know the gossip.

The words that came out my mouth sounded muffled in my head. The sound resonated as if someone else were saying them. "I got them." Those were the only three syllables that I could seem to muster to indicate that I did grab our paychecks. I also managed to grab a few personal items off of my desk to shove into my purse.

Shell-shocked is what the state is called. But it is also my MO when dealing with emergencies. A peaceful calm settles in my psyche. Inside my brain, there is no screaming or panic. Calm comes as a civil "matter of fact" reaction that takes over my soul when an emergency arises. Panic would use valuable seconds that I need to evaluate a course of action.

On this particularly beautiful day, the sun shone into my corner office from large, westward-facing windows. The Colorado Rockies were visible, with a vast blue sky showing off the snow-capped peaks. The sea of blue held a few puffy clouds that were dancing above the mountains. My cherry wood desk and credenza would belong to someone else when I left the premises. The new person would never realize that this furniture set, purchased for me, had sentimental value. They would sit there later today to ponder problems that the view from the windows would help to solve.

I was in disbelief—thrown out of my own company. Calling the police wasn't necessary. The phone call was a statement meant to show the employees left behind that someone new was now in charge. There could be no other reason to call the police, because we were exiting peacefully. Neither this takeover nor our forced exit was written in our corporate bylaws. The asshole wanted to make a statement that *I* was the bad guy. *I* was the cause of dismay for the whole industry to see; that is why the men in blue were necessary. The show of force was meant to imply that I might cause a scene exiting the corporation.

> **Desperation almost always leads to fatal results.**

David, our oldest son and the company's IT wiz, stood frozen as if he were a statue grounded in cement. Fresh out of the Marine Corps, he was used to not knowing every detail of a situation when it came to corporate America. In the Marines, he knew not to question authority. Still, he wondered, "Are the police here for me, too?" He also asked, "Mom, will you go to jail?" A flash of a toddler passed before my eyes. Wasn't it just yesterday that he was scared something may happen to his mother and he would be lost? Like the time he wandered away in the department store?

"No, David, you were not fired, or asked to leave." I hugged him. "Stay, no matter how hard it is, unless they tell you to go. We need to figure out what happened, and what we are going to do." I gave a small chuckle. "And no—no one will be hauled to jail." He looked scared, much like he did when he left for Marine boot camp. Fear caused his red hair to take on a more scarlet color against his darkening freckles. The effect made him look much younger.

There was a cardboard box packed for both of us— me as president and my husband Rich as vice president.

The traitors had prepared small parcels filled with valuable mementos. The offering was their farewell to the founders. They neglected to insert my cherished plant and wouldn't release it even when I asked. This was another sentimental item I was leaving behind. The staff had sent me the plant as part of their condolence over the loss of my Dad only months before. The foliage now belonged to the traitors. A stupid plant had no value to them. Withholding the potted greenery was a spiteful move that they knew would be a knife wound.

I was deemed guilty. Shamefaced, I wanted to hide under a rock. We were guilty of ignorance mainly; without the knowledge that we needed documents to protect ourselves from our partner. Oh, if only Google had been as formidable then as it is today. We would have known our rights to prevent this from happening. Don had become an unpleasant partner as soon as we signed over 51 percent of the company's stock for his $250,000 investment. The company needed the money desperately. Desperation almost always leads to fatal results. The outcome most assuredly was deadly in this case.

The Board of Directors consisted of me, Rich, Don, and Matt. Matt was the controller that Don inserted as soon as he received his certificate of ownership. The tied vote to have Rich and I resign broke with his 51 percent. "Resignation" had a softer sound than "fired," but the result was the same. Both terms came with humiliation, shock, and resentment.

Blame and anger filled my mind on the day I was forced out of my company. *I am the founder, the inventor.* My guts remained engraved in the company. The client satisfaction and work flow was successful...heck, *I* was successful, so how did it get this far away from me? Part of the answer lay with Rich.

At first, Don was kind, helpful, and believed in me. I needed him because I took the ride of chance with Rich and we failed. Rich was a high risk-taker. All growth takes risks, of course, but he was too risky, and look where that gamble got us. The company grew too fast, without a solid business plan, and was in debt. The only way to get the capital was to make a deal with the devil himself. So I made a deal, not knowing Don was the devil. I was angry at Rich for putting me in the position to have to get Satan involved, but I was mad at Don for rising up from the dark forces.

I felt that Matt was a competent controller and CPA. He was young and motivated. His father was a lawyer, Don's best friend. Never mind the sirens ablaze in my head at the time; the company needed a money man. Rich had handled the finances that had brought us to the position in which we found ourselves now. So apparently that wasn't a good plan. New methods were needed. The company needed a manager that could keep track of the hundreds of Benjamins coming and going.

In the end, we walked out with our small boxes while the staff, *our* staff, looked on in disbelief. We heard crying from some as they stayed entombed in their workstations. Other employees followed us out the door with the police and vowed never to return. These brave employees linked arms to come with us wherever we would go next. Even though we carried a copy of our non-compete that stated we could not operate within 50 miles of our former company, these people believed in us. We would contest this document, if only we could afford a lawyer.

We drove to a motel precisely 50 miles away to set up shop, to obey the verbiage of the non-compete. On the drive, my mind twirled in many directions. There was still anger at Rich for putting us in this financial position in the first place. Commitment also came into play in the decision to start the company over and to have Rich involved in the process. There were too many years and struggles between Rich and me to give up on the marriage. The auto industry was my birthright. Cars became my adopted DNA early on; I felt they had been predestined for me. Heading down the same path with Rich and a company felt like déjà vu. I was worried that this would be another mistake.

> **Within an hour, we started a new business with nothing more than lint in our pockets.**

Once in the motel room the appropriate distance away, we found the only lawyer we could afford to set up the new company. Never mind that Greg was prominently known as the lawyer to the porn stars. He was more than happy to have a legitimate client to add to his repertoire. I was delighted we found counsel so quickly.

Out loud, I said to myself, "If Greg could help the porn industry, well; the car business isn't that far off in scruples." How fitting this scene was: we were doing business in a motel with a porn star lawyer. I was glad that Dad couldn't see me, but I still wanted my plant back.

The motel room consisted of two queen beds with soft, noisy mattresses. Ugly striped bedspreads covered the rickety beds. These we quickly removed before sitting on them. Looking at the headboard from the side view in the light, we could see handprints where someone used them to steady his or her body during recreational activities. Those smudges left no doubt as to what went on in the bed. That thought had goose bumps traveling up my arm, and a gag reaction involuntarily came up in my throat.

> **A desire to succeed is worth more than money.**

I needed to be able to sit cross-legged on the bed to do my paperwork without that visual, so I suppressed both reactions. By the window, there was a small, wobbly table and a single chair. Rich took to spreading papers on the table to call clients; he was a master at enticing business to come our way. One needed to be conscious when going to the bathroom not to flush during a sales call. The sound of the toilet may cause a new sale to go right down the drain.

Within an hour, we started a new business with nothing more than lint in our pockets. We came with a desire to succeed, which is worth more than money. The next day, our company personnel grew by 50 percent, as Don's firing of David allowed him to join us in the new venture.

Most successful people have gone broke, been destitute, and have gotten back up to drive on and do it again. In fact, most have been bankrupt more than once. If I can fail and get back up, so can you. It probably feels like the end of the world to you, but if you get some sleep, you can begin a new day.

**Lesson Learned:** Professional drivers don't let non-fatal mistakes keep them from driving again.

BUCKLE UP FOR BUSINESS SUCCESS

Motel room with ugly bedspreads

# CHAPTER 3

# Victimitis

*"With everything that has happened
to you, you can either feel sorry for
yourself or treat what has happened as
a gift. Everything is either an opportunity
to grow or an obstacle to keep you
from growing. You get to choose."*

—Dr. Wayne W. Dyer

Our culture is full of victims. These are the people who have an excuse not to make something of themselves. They need to feel like they are being held down for some reason, to create some explanation of why they cannot move on. Being kicked out of my own business could have made me feel like a victim, but instead, we picked ourselves up and started fresh.

Other situations could make you feel like a victim. You might have a bad home life or marriage that you let keep you from succeeding.

My husband was a recovering drug addict and alcoholic. Throughout our marriage, we have had a rollercoaster of a life. He used to drink to sleep, but that doesn't work out so well. He poured a big glass of vodka at bedtime and passed out with his 16-ounce pink tumbler residing neatly on a coaster on his bedside table.

Snuggled as he was under a clean down comforter, the smell of fresh scented detergent should have whisked him into REM sleep, but dreams eluded him. Rich would wake up a couple of hours later, pour another tumbler full, and then pass out again. That cycle repeated until he was pouring an eight-ounce glass around 6 a.m., then waking up to go to work at 8 a.m. fully loaded. He awoke wobbling much like a child's egged-shaped Weeble toy.

His drinking hit hard one morning, when he could not even walk straight and was attempting to drive to work and I could not stop him from getting behind the wheel. I called David to come to talk him down and get him back into bed. "Dad," David reasoned with him calmly, "I can handle clients. Besides, the people you are calling need their computer access setup. That is what my job is, and I'm good at it. Let me do this today, and you can be good as new tomorrow." There was arguing, pleading, but finally, we got him back into bed to sleep it off.

> **Just because things get tough doesn't give you an excuse to bail out of anything.**

Our daughter was still in high school and decided this was a chance to skip class since we had a crisis. Changing back into her jammies, she announced, "I'll just stay home today since there are problems." I made a statement that changed her life and one she still remembers: "Just because things get tough doesn't give you an excuse to bail out of anything. Bad things make us stronger and more determined than ever to succeed. Now get your butt to school and while you're at it—get an A in math!"

If you let problems prevent you from functioning, then issues will keep compounding until you get an Itis. An Itis is an inflammatory state of the mind where destructive patterns keep you in a rut of doing the same crap over and over again.

You have to get over an Itis. There is no pill to take for it, no magic drug. The school of hard knocks can heal it if you want to recover. Some people have an Itis forever, preferring to take the road of accepting to live with the disease.

My beginnings were not perfect. If I had paid attention

to statistics, it would appear that I had every reason in the world to fail. The facts stacked up hard against my success.

> **An Itis is an inflammatory state of the mind where destructive patterns keep you in a rut of doing the same crap over and over again.**

I was an orphan with no family, left alone in a hospital nursery until a family adopted me. My new parents wanted me and gave me a sense of belonging. They were strangers who took the chance and gambled on what was hiding inside this child's soul and genetics. Mom and Dad assured me that I was predestined for success; all I had to do was never to give up, and believe I could do it.

There have been times when I felt lonely and unwanted, and generally as though I did not belong. You might not be an orphan, but you and I have a lot in common, with similar sentiments from time to time.

I have warts and have experienced many roadblocks, just like you. Courage is what we muster to rise above those hurdles.

Refusing to listen to negative voices or labels, I choose to overcome all challenges and accept all hands offered to me, continuing to be grateful for every leg up. I know to never waste the effort of others, and this has been the secret ingredient for a worthy life.

Time after time, I dismissed the inner voices telling me I am going to fail. I replaced the negative chirping with the sweet voice of victory, encouraging myself to keep moving. We are God's children, and He calls us to be victorious. He doesn't put us on earth to be failures. He wants to bless us with immeasurable success, but we have to do the work.

Because of the disaster we experienced after we were kicked out of our business, we now own three profitable companies. Our life is full, with four children, five grandchildren, and a marriage that has withstood 40 years. I have good health and almost anything desired in life. Everyday I have gratitude for the ups and downs in my life. I express the thanks by giving back to others. Gratitude is an expression of being thankful, but an abundance of thanks for your blessings can only be expressed by giving back to others. Being charitable with my time and finances provides me fulfillment that cannot be felt by merely "making it" up the business ladder. Once you make it to the top rung on the ladder, hop off and help others get there too; that is how to express gratitude.

Automotive Warranty Network is a $22 million company, with over 200 employees and over 800 car dealerships as clients. We serve as a third-party administrator, recovering money from the manufacturer for repairs performed on vehicles by the dealership. We deal with all legal aspects of the manufacturer's audit process, and train service advisors, technicians, and service managers. I am a woman who has been working in a man's world for over 30 years.

Our House Properties owns several short-term rentals in the ski resort of Breckenridge. I manage those as well as own them, producing several hundred thousand dollars a year of income while maintaining five-star ratings in quality and customer service.

Our House Publications is my author platform, where I have written and published five award-winning and bestselling children's picture books, and one non-fiction memoir to date.

I have a blessed life, and stand a conqueror over Victimitis. For me, I never felt like a victim, because seeing beyond the past allows one to see the future. This attitude was an antiviral mask of protection that was part of my gift of life, and here is what it said: "Get your butt up, girl! You can't do anything sitting in the mud!"

> **There's another chapter in front of you, but you have to be willing to take the next step.**

There is a particular verse I love that reminds me that I am not a victim. "For I know the plans I have for you," declares the LORD, "plans to prosper you and not to harm you, plans to give you hope and a future."(Jeremiah 29:11)

It means stop looking at the bad so that you can see the good coming.

Here's the key: when you go through a disappointment, when you go through a loss, don't stop on that page in your life. You have to decide to keep moving forward. There's another chapter in front of you, but you have to be willing to take the next step. Sometimes, we get so focused on what didn't work out that we stay stuck, reliving the disappointment. If that's you, recognize that you've been on that page long enough. It's time to let it go and turn the page.

I have it all for now. How did I get here? What collateral damage was left behind? How can *you* get here, as well?

We all have hard beginnings. Some may be born into ghettos, unwanted by parents. Some are raised poor, without money. There are babies born with deformities, mental holdbacks, premature births, and they get a slow start to life. Yes, even the well-to-do have it hard, because they don't know what it means to want for success. Life wasn't perfect for me; if I can make it, so can you.

. . . . . . . . . . . . . . . . . . . . . . . . . . . . . . . . . . . . . . . . . . . .

**Lesson Learned:** Throw that darn word "victim" out the window. There is no whining if you want to race with the big guys.

My adoption and Dad

# CHAPTER 4

# Court

*"Insider: a person who has access
to confidential information."*

Now to get back to the story of our company after being removed, starting over, and being sued. We headed to court. We were not done fighting for our right to form another business.

Our attorney paced up and down the hall of the courthouse on his short, squatty legs chanting, "Oh, it's not good. Not good. The judge's face had pensive frown lines. I've seen that look before. We're not winning." He began wringing his hands as he repeated the sentence. His lips puckered with every sound of dread that came from his mouth.

Rich and I sat on the benches in the hallway where we waited as the judge decided the verdict. The seats were hard, the floor cold, and the echo of the great hallway impressed upon the seriousness of our fate. We had been silently praying as Greg paced the hall. He was dressed in a cheap tweed suit that was too short, even for him. He continued talking to himself as we sat. For me, the praying gave me an emotional place to go that kept panic at bay.

At some point, Porn Man started trying to reassure himself by repeating, "OK, OK, it's OK. OK, it's going to be OK. OK." He sounded a bit like Joe Pesci playing Leo Getz in the *Lethal Weapon* movies. I remember at one point, I let a little giggle loose as I finished my prayer with an *Amen*.

> "Everything I know I learned from reading those books."

My testimony in court had consisted of only answering questions with a yes or no answer up to this point. Questions asked by our freaked-out attorney and opposing counsel had been phrased for a quick response. The entire non-compete contract hinged on the fact that as the founder, I had trade secrets in the automotive field that no one else possessed.

My brain housed enormous amounts of information on the automobile industry. However, the information that I possessed was available to anyone who cared to read the automotive policy manuals. The reason I possessed the "secrets" is that I read every piece of published data in each manual. Reading was something no one else in the company had been willing to do. All one needed to do was to study the manufacturer's published materials to gather the same knowledge that I held.

At the cross-examination, I entered the courtroom with armloads of thick books that the court entered as evidence. I saw the opposing council stir nervously and talk to each other behind cupped hands.

The direct question posed to me by our lawyer was, "Do you have trade secrets that give you insider knowledge?" To answer, I only needed to point at the manuals that I had made available as evidence. As I pointed my voice softly answered, "No. Everything I know I learned from reading those books." I continued and gave excerpts from published instructions straight from the manufacturers' materials.

I heard a whisper from the opposition's lawyer—"Is that true? Do you know what is in the manual?" I saw Matt shake his head "no," followed by a shrug. No more questions came from their team on the cross examination.

Testimony completed, we vacated the room for the verdict.

> **"Do you know what is in the manual?"**

## BUCKLE UP FOR BUSINESS SUCCESS

The wait wasn't long, despite our Joe Pesci lawyer wearing out the tiles outside the courtroom. Rich and I re-entered the court chamber together with our poor attorney, whose sweat showed about the armpits through his suit coat. There was a silent stillness as His Honor announced, "The non-compete has no relevance in this case. Mrs. Reinicke obtained all knowledge from published information that is free to all contractors associated with individual manufacturers. She is free to compete as it fits her location. Court adjourned."

Don, Matt, and their legal team sat, not moving in their chairs. Their tailored suits looked ordinary, wrinkled from the day. The verdict was a blow they were not expecting, and one they immediately regretted. Our sole legal counsel needed a paper bag to blow into, due to the hyperventilation he was experiencing. Small bursts came from him between breaths. "We won? We won! I won? OK. It's OK. OK. I won." He hunched over, trying to catch his breath. His words came out high-pitched. True to his industry roots, he breathed out some "F" word exclamations, while we looked heavenward and whispered, "Thank You."

The employees, who came with us from the other company, were also in the court. They shouted their hurrahs, pumping their fists into the air. Rich and I smiled and readied our move from the sleazy motel to the basement of our home just minutes from what was now Don and Matt's business.

Walking out of court, I felt a cold hand on my shoulder

and turned; it was the solicitor for the opposition, Matt's father. He stood looking at my face as he asked me to come back to the company fold. He explained, "We only wanted Rich's resignation. Matt was instructed to refuse to accept your resignation, but in the heat of the moment, the conversations didn't go as planned. The company wishes to offer you reinstitution as if this matter never happened."

I laughed, then I giggled, and finally I managed a polite, "No, thank you." Involuntarily, my head shook side to side, and my chuckling continued as my team walked from the building, down the steps, and out to our vehicle. Wind blew my hair and I felt like one of the stars in *Law and Order* after a win.

There was no time to waste. We were all hungry to get to work and kick the competition's ass. I had taken a beating, and now I was going to dish one out with one hell of a team delivering the main course.

**Lesson Learned:** Professional drivers don't let hardships ruin the race.

BUCKLE UP FOR BUSINESS SUCCESS

The courthouse

# CHAPTER 5

# Work Ethic

*"Work ethic: The principle that hard work is intrinsically virtuous or worthy of reward."*

My first lessons on ethical behavior came from the school of hard knocks. At the tender age of 15, I decided to learn to drive a clutch vehicle from a teenage boy. Never mind that I didn't have a driver's license. Thinking I had all the knowledge I needed under my belt, I took a corner too quickly. I had the clutch pushed in without downshifting.

Six teenagers packed into a stick shift VW Bug were laughing, shouting, and having a great adventure. As I turned the wheel, we tipped over onto the side as the car took the curve. It was almost a soft tip, not even doing much damage to the Beetle. With no one hurt, the laughing started up again as we all gathered around to set the small Bug back up on its wheels. As we were about to get rolling, the police showed up. They were quick to issue tickets to each of us.

The ticket carried a court appearance, with my parents present, for careless driving and driving without a license. There was no easy way to break the news to Mom and Dad and finding the right moment to do so was imperative. Volunteering to comb my mom's hair was a gracious act, so I chose that moment, making my announcement in a cloud of hairspray. I was sure that fog from the hairspray would lighten the writing on the ticket.

I can still see her face as she read the ticket. Her black hair was still ratted up and she had a towel around her shoulders to keep the spray off her clothes. For a moment she was silent, but as the reality sunk in, she started screaming for my Dad to come in. "Buster. Buster, come in here. Look what your child has done!"

> **"The 'Hushpuppy' express is pulling up, so you best get on it."**

The ticket meant a fine that I would have to pay. Dad felt the accident also revealed that their teen had too much time on her hands and needed a job. He suggested I try the

Safeway supermarket right down the street, because they were in need of baggers. He offered, "The 'Hushpuppy' express is pulling up, so you best get on it and head right down to the store to apply." They hired me right away, and I was due to report for work the minute school was out every day.

The job was hard and the more work they gave me, the more I excelled. I hated to be idle. During downtime, the store put me in charge of sorting the sticky pop bottles into the proper crates. Coke bottles needed to fill each hole in the cartons for Coca-Cola, as did Pepsi bottles in the cartons for Pepsi. My favorites were the gooey bottles of Orange Crush. It was like a puzzle, a game of concentration, and I loved it. This job was recycling basics. The glass bottles were sent back to the factory to be washed, sanitized, refilled and resold. Bottles didn't go into a landfill or made into anything else.

> **Nothing good comes from boredom. It's said that idle hands are the devil's workshop, an old saying dating at least as far back as Chaucer in the 12thcentury.**

Summer was on the horizon, and Dad had the foresight to know that filling my hours could either be with mischief or more work. The saying, "Idle hands are the devil's workshop," was his motto. He was the zone manager for Chrysler, and he had many dealerships under his territory. Channeling my fascination with cars to working in the dealerships seemed a logical step.

One of his dealers a few blocks away from our home was looking for a cashier in service. Offering me as an employee, Dad stated, "If she's good, you can keep her; if she's not… fire her ass." He knew all along I would have too much grit to be fired.

Problem solved for that summer—working two jobs with no time to get into trouble except on weekends. Choosing not to stand still or stay home, I started modeling clothing on the weekends and at nights. There were times when there was a rush to get the sweet soda wash off in time to put on a fancy dress for the photographers' deadlines. Dad was happy, I was happy, and trouble was at bay that summer.

The poor judgment I used in rolling the Bug forced me into a situation of working hard, having integrity, and using my talents wisely. These were lessons that I have never forgotten and use everyday. My Dad taught me a valuable lesson: *if you make a mistake, own it—then fix it. Don't make it again.*

Losing the company was much like rolling that Beetle—a terrible misjudgment that had me digging back into my roots to correct the cause of the problem. Rebuilding is a time to focus: live to do the work. Spend every hour, even the ones eating and sleeping, on the company. Whatever is needed is what you have to do to get the job done.

**Lesson Learned:** Racing consumes a driver's thoughts, dreams, and actions. He or she lives to race. His or her home is the vehicle.

BUCKLE UP FOR BUSINESS SUCCESS

Dad knew that following the family in the automotive industry would give me a good living. A picture of my grandfather on the left and my dad next to him.

# CHAPTER 6

# Automotive Warranty Network is Born

*"Look for the bare necessities,
the simple bare necessities."*

— From The Jungle Book
by Rudyard Kipling

Our new office was in the basement of our home. It was a space with bare cement floors, concrete walls, and single exposed light bulbs hanging from the ceiling with a pull chain. In other words, our new office was dark, dingy, and sparse. To add to that, we had no money to equip it, but we did have our computers, and that was all we needed to make money. We had employees, clients, power, and determination to make the business a success. Plus, the basement was a step up from the motel room. At least our new digs didn't have hidden DNA fit for a crime scene.

Begging for hand-me-downs was not beneath us. We spread the word throughout our church that we would take any old desks, chairs, and lamps that people wanted to offload. Old metal desks came pouring in. They were the heavy kind that weighed 300 pounds. Once those suckers were down in the basement, they were never coming out. I could hear the wives of the church Elders encouraging their husbands in a most Christian-like voice, "I think it is a wonderful idea taking that ugly desk in your office to the Reinicke's to use in their new business. You can get the other nine Elders to help you carry it over there, too! Our house will miss the old dinosaur."

> **Actually putting in the work to get to the goal takes effort.**

Our new space soon had wires looped over exposed ceiling beams. The conduits led to multiple phone lines coming into the house. The wires made our backyard look like CIA headquarters. Our company had a new name: Automotive Warranty Network. Moreover, it had 12 dedicated people to make it a success. Wanting to be a success and being willing to do whatever it takes to succeed are two different visualizations. *Wanting* is just the desire to have an accomplishment. *<u>Actually putting in the work</u>* to get to the goal takes effort.

We borrowed $5,000 from a friend to cover the equipment we needed to get going. Boy, we sure hated to ask for money from anyone. Once our first billing was complete, we immediately gave the money back. Borrowing money is the fastest way to lose a friend. Have class—always pay the money back as soon as you can, especially if it's from a friend.

> **Financing your receivables means you are paying interest to use your own money.**

Another thing we learned is that financing receivables would be a costly way to do business. The financing would charge us to use our own money. However, when you are just starting out, it is necessary to have the money that you billed your client quickly. Waiting for payment means that you don't have capital to work with. To eliminate this expense, we adopted a policy that billed our clients twice a month for cash flow. We did our billing on the 15$^{th}$ and end of the month, then scheduled payroll on the 10$^{th}$ and 25$^{th}$ of the month. This allowed time for payments to come in before cutting our payroll checks. The theory would work once the ball started rolling.

Another incentive for quick payments from our clients was to offer a three percent discount for payments received within five working days of the invoice. Bi-monthly billing is a practice we still use today, and we never have clients contest our policy. The result is constant cash flow to support growth without having to take out a loan.

> **Hmmm…I wonder if there's a connection between hard work, miracles, and gratitude.**

Our first billing was exciting and relatively light, given our setback with the time that court took away from our labors. Our employees knew how tight money was going to be and knew there could be a delay in their paychecks. They knew we prayed every morning for not only our finances, but we begged God to supply their "daily bread" too.

We had two chairs in our bedroom that we called our prayer chairs, where Rich and I sat every morning to lay out our hearts and needs to God. There is nothing like hardships to bring you to your knees. We experienced what we knew were miracles, and every day we gave praise for what our hands held. We were never alone, because the heavens constantly showed its hands as we worked.

Hmmm...I wonder if there's a connection between hard work, miracles, and gratitude?

As our first payday came upon us, we needed that miracle. Our bank was a local bank that we had used at our prior company. Rich would drive downtown daily to deposit our meager funds. We had purchased a cranberry-colored 2000 Dodge Intrepid prior to our departure from the previous company, and already the vehicle was exhibiting head gasket problems. Rich kept his fingers crossed the darn thing would start when he was done at the bank with every trip he made.

Rich saw the bank manager as he entered and shook his hand with a smile. That day, of all days, the manager happened to ask, "Tell me about how things are going. I hear you set up shop and already have deposits."

Rich smiled and answered, "Things are good. We have employees and clients. Work is pouring in. We are working hard. It's going to be a success. Every day is a new opportunity. Man, this breakup was a blessing in disguise. We have always wanted to give a broader service to our customers and now we are able to."

> "I could do a line of credit for $10,000 right now."

The banker slapped him on the back. "That is great to hear. Glad you're coming out on top. Now if there's anything you need, let me know."

Wow—there it was—an invitation from The Almighty. Just like in the movies, angels sang, bells rang, and sun lit up the sky. Rich jumped on it. "Since you're asking, our payroll is tomorrow, and we could use a little cash coverage while our clients send in their checks this first complete billing."

"Well, let me see now, I could do a line of credit for $10,000 right now if that works for you?" The banker offered.

Rich choked on his spit and could not breathe or speak; all he managed to do was nod his head up and down, up and down, and up and down.

With the deal complete, he took a pen and filled out checks while sitting in the maroon Dodge before he ever left the parking lot. His hand shaking, he completed the amount and added his signature. There was a water stain on the last paper that came from a tear that escaped out of overwhelming relief.

Once he arrived back to our basement office, he handed out checks to everyone while each employee cried as they chimed in unison, "We believe in miracles!"

One administrator fell to his knees on the cold stone floor and bawled like a baby, "Oh, please don't stop praying. I needed money. Let's have cash every payday."

> **Guts, grit, and determination assisted in the process of success, but without faith they could have been useless.**

Guts, grit, and determination assisted in the process of success, but without faith they could have been useless.

We learned that those who don't ask don't get, but knock and the door shall be opened.

---

**Lesson Learned:** Every race driver has a miracle near-miss to tell about.

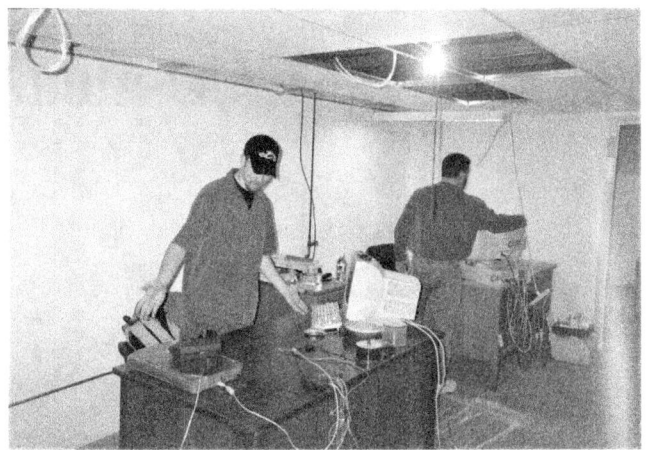

Picture of the basement which was our new office

# CHAPTER 7

# You'll Never Grow Alone

*"The key to growth is acknowledging your
fear of the unknown and jumping in anyway."*

— *Jen Sincero*

As both the old and new companies grew, I said to myself countless times, "If I don't do this part of the job, what the heck am I going to do? I can't let my administrators do all the administration; I must process these claims myself."

I'll be darned. Who would have known that I was not the center of the universe? Indeed, I thought I was the mainstay of the whole company. However, the moment I stopped working claims, I found the time to manage the department. As the growth continued, I hired a production manager. My conversations with myself resurfaced. That nagging voice, "I must control these people myself; what if my manager does it wrong? Anyway, what am I going to do if I don't manage people?"

Again, to my surprise, I found I didn't have time to manage anymore. I was too busy training people all month. It didn't take much time to figure out that the company needed a full-time trainer. By the time the new company expanded, I only whispered in my head instead of talking out loud to myself. That soft sound blew in my ear, "What the heck am I going to do if I don't work claims, don't manage, and can't train?"

> **As your business grows, you will need to work upward.**

So now I am sure you get my drift that the fear of *not being needed* is a growth stopper. The concern of stepping aside will cause you to stunt the growth of the company. Being constantly in the way of your people will keep them from reaching their full potential. You most probably will lose the good ones because they will quit. You will be leading the company by fear instead of confidence.

These powerful resonating fears tell you:

> *Well, no one can do it as good as me.*
> *We don't have money for that right now.*
> *I have to keep doing all the work for it to be done right.*
> *Everything will be screwed up.*
> *My clients will not be happy clients without me.*

> **The fear of "not being needed" is a growth stopper.**

These fears are lies.

To grow, there is always the next step. I know it costs money; it is expensive. Moreover, there's this truth: no one will do it as well as you—at first. Some of the employees have never done the job before, so it is going to take time for them to learn. They will learn either through mistakes or by excellent teaching.

There is planning that you can do that will help with these fears and worries. Working upward will move your business forward, sometimes at a speed that you never imagined!

Let's address the next steps. All small businesses start with the owner, creator, and founder doing every aspect of the job. You have to because it is your baby and you don't have the capital to hire staff. Babies need care—your infant company is no different. You have to nurture it, feed it, change its poopie pants, and—most importantly—you will lose sleep…lots of it. You will stay up all hours of the night either worrying or laboring to make the company flourish.

As the baby grows into a toddler, you have to help it start to move on its own. Helping the company to be ambulatory is the baby step phase, where ideas and productions begin to develop. Now you are busy chasing the walking toddler, keeping it out of trouble. Others are starting to work for you, and you feel like you're cleaning up messes, but, in reality, you are teaching. Your business is learning how to do things from you.

> **The teen years are hell in business.**

An excellent example of this comes from my property business. I hired a woman to do the cleaning for my short-term rentals. At first, I worked beside her to teach her how I wanted things done. Then she began to do an excellent job on her own. She did a great job and began to think like me, noticing items that needed attention all on her own. She didn't need me to clean alongside her anymore. I could then focus on decorating, repairing, and hospitality.

It's not long before you have to start allowing your employees more freedom to grow. The development comes in additional duties, and then finally allowing them to develop ingenuity. This growth is as scary as the teen years, because they might find opportunities for trouble.

With my children, the teen years ranged from that compliant child all the way to the opposite end of the spectrum with the wildest child. The fact that each offspring was different meant that his or her boundaries would be defined differently. The analogy is much the same with employees. Some of your staff will merit an increase in salary, and some will not work for you very long. The teen years are hell in business.

Let's go back to the same example with the property company. As the business grew, I started giving the cleaner, Lee, new duties. Lee then elevated her status to become the property manager. She cleaned, made small repairs, and used her creativity to rearrange and decorate. Uh-oh! Her style was different from mine, so I had to set some boundaries to navigate this growth period. She would take pictures to send me before purchasing new or replacement items. Soon she learned my taste and was able to use her creativity within a process we set up.

Some instances may arise where employees take the easy route or opt not to engage in their own growth. I love the saying, *what are you doing to make yourself better?* Rather than *what are others doing for you?*

> **What are you doing to make yourself better?**

I fell victim to this latter way of thinking at the beginning of my career. I was working at a Chrysler dealership that offered to promote me to warranty administrator. My father was the zone warranty manager of the entire Western zone. He knew the policy and answers to all the ins and outs of warranty. It was my Dad who taught me one of my best business lessons.

In my new job, I didn't have the expertise to submit a claim for a complicated vehicle repair. Knowing there was a family resource, I decided that dear ole Dad, the zone manager for Chrysler, would know the answer. I called dear old Dad.

> **Dear ole Dad hung up on me.**

"Hi, Dad. I have a hard question on this claim. I don't know how to submit for this type of repair. Can you tell me how to do it?" I sweetly quizzed him.

On the other end of the phone, I could hear him take a drag of his cigarette. I pictured him sitting at his desk, dressed to kill in his Johnny Carson suit, ready to give me the information I needed. After exhaling a cloud of smoke, he asked me a question in return. "What page of the manual are you on?" I heard another inhale of smoke being sucked into his lungs.

My mouth fell open to answer, but no sound came out. I had neglected to have my policy manual out, much less have it open to find the answer on my own. Finally, I stuttered, "Uh, I don't have a page number." Immediately and without warning, there was a *click* and then the buzz of the dead phone line. Dear ole Dad hung up on me, which I can assure you made him chuckle. Dad knew that if he answered, he would be working harder to fix my problem than I was willing to work fixing my problem.

From then on, I devoured anything I could read. Not only to look for answers, but to engross myself into learning my craft. I begged for classes that were available and even offered to pay for them on my own. The books would be my vehicle for success and went home with me as reading material for the bathroom. When all else failed, I contacted hotlines and other administrators for information. What I gleaned from doing my own research was that not all people would give you the correct answers; you have to double-check them and look information up yourself. Only believe what you can prove.

We continue to tell this story to all our new employees. Your employees need to understand that ultimately their growth is in their own hands.

> **Only believe what you can prove.**

I didn't know why I went through the pain of growth until the time came for me to empathize with others during their pain. Often, being able to tell my story has helped our staff understand their own process to move up in the company. Leaving a position that you love and do well in is scary. Anytime you take a chance on the next job, you don't know if you're going to be good at the task or not. I had learning curves, times that I lost sleep to figure out what I needed to do, and times I cried due to frustration. In your company, the people you choose to elevate will have those same feelings.

---

**Lesson Learned:** A racecar driver never lets fear sabotage his or her potential or the need for speed.

# CHAPTER 8

# Whale Tails

*"Somebody once said that in looking for people to hire, you look for three qualities: integrity, intelligence, and energy. And if you don't have the first, the other two will kill you. You think about it; it's true. If you hire somebody without integrity, you really want them to be dumb and lazy."*

— *Warren Buffett*

It took only a few months for the new business to boom. We filled the basement with bodies and moved some employees into our den and extra bedroom. Cringing at my home's mutilation, I covered my ears and closed my eyes as Rich and David drilled holes in my beautiful hardwood floors. The holes facilitated phone lines and computer cables for the new business coming in. I reminded myself that growing is a blessing, as every drill sound meant another demolition to the hickory flooring. Finally, there was nowhere else to put bodies or computers. The wonderful old wood floor looked like Swiss cheese with all the holes that had been drilled. It was time to spend money on an office. Oh, how I hated to let loose of the hard-earned money for rent. I was fearful we would overspend and be back to where we were with the other company. Too much, too fast—going broke.

Rich, still the risk-taker, and me, the nickel-squeezer, needed to find a compromise. We found an older office building where the rent was acceptable. The building aesthetics would not have been conducive for visitors. There was creaking on the uneven floors and toilets that rocked every time you perched on the throne.

The outside looked much like an old one-bedroom apartment building that someone decided to make into office space. But entertaining clients was not part of our business model, and the purpose of having an office was to have places for those two-ton desks to reside.

> **Covering the better Bs for success—
> boobs, butts, and bellies.**

Finding good people is always a crapshoot. We decided to get some help from a local employment agency. The agency sent representatives who were friendly enough as they arrived with smiles. However, the woman that was helping us leaned forward, and her dang butt crack hung out of her pants. Her booty was showing, big as life and twice as ugly, staring at me as I entered the room. Not only could you see her big old butt crack, but her "whale tail" thong sticking up there as well. It was not a pretty sight.

Right there, I shuffled them out the door, thanking them for their assistance. I explained that people who don't have enough common sense to dress for success couldn't be trusted to find personnel with any sense at all.

I call this "covering the better *B*s of success." We still post it in our employee manual.

> *Make sure it's covered:*
> *Boobs*
> *Butts*
> *Bellies*

Dressing for success isn't everything, though. Finding people who are presentable doesn't always mean they have a lick of common sense beneath that exterior. Such was the case with Karla. Karla looked the part of a bright and eager candidate. She interviewed well, smiled a lot, was easy to get along with, and we knew she would be a teachable student.

Karla nodded her head and wrote instructions down which gave us confidence that her work would be exemplary. Boy, were we fooled!

Our company is responsible for entering correct data for the vehicle manufacturers in the manner they request. One particular manufacturer had a demand for inserting the technician, the customer phone number, and service advisor into the claim. The manufacturer used this information to perform customer follow-up calls. The computer system did not have a field for this information programmed into the format. The manufacturer insisted that the data show as an equation on the first line of the document.

> **People who are presentable don't always have a lick of common sense.**

Karla, the bright student, diligently wrote down the equation so she would not forget. First, you put the number sign [#], then the tech number. Next, the equal sign [=] followed by the customer phone number. Finally, the [@] followed by the advisor number. The first line should look something like this: #1234=5554443333@2272.

Karla's computer skills were quick, and she could enter claims faster than anyone in our office. We thought we had a home run hitter in her.

About a month later, there was a call from one of our

dealers. "The manufacturer is not receiving our customer information. None of the technician numbers or customer phone numbers are there. We are getting no customer service awards," the dealer informed us.

I assured him the equation was being entered on the first line of every claim and could he check to see what was on the first line that the manufacturer received. Sure enough, it was right there on the document, precisely as Karla wrote it down: "#tech=phone number@advisor." The problem was, she never put in the actual, individual information.

That was forgivable and laughable. Okay, that job was above Karla's skill level. As a valued employee, we switched her job to receptionist and charged her with keeping the petty cash drawer. She had a terrific phone voice and a willing spirit. She was also very honest, so we knew she would not steal or mismanage cash.

Her instructions were not to give anyone cash. I remember the day well. I had several packages to get out in the mail and needed cash to get to the post office. "Hey, Karla. Why don't you give me a $20 just in case and I will run to the post office. I will bring back the difference." Karla tilted her head and hugged the cash drawer, "No one can have any cash, though."

I explained patiently, "It's OK, Karla. The cash is my cash because I own the company."

Karla's final mistake was hoarding the drawer and not permitting me, the owner, to have access to the petty cash to pay for postage. I grabbed the cash drawer and broke it open. Then I fired her.

**Lesson Learned:** It's imperative to have a good-looking race car, but it's what's under the hood that will win the race.

# CHAPTER 9

# Business is Business

*"Making a great icing means that you must have a cake to spread the icing on."*

The reason people start a business is that they are exceptional at their craft. Whatever it is—they are the best at it. Great chefs are passionate about opening their own restaurant. Fashionista's put together the best boutiques. I was the best administrator in the business. A key ingredient for success is to be better at your craft than anyone else is. The craft is the start of your business, but I have witnessed many companies with a great crafter gurgle down the drain. I compare the craft as the tasty icing on the cake. When you eat the icing it is wonderful, but eventually you reach the cake part. The cake is the flour, butter, eggs, and everything else—without that, there won't be anything to put the icing on.

After the fiasco with our previous company, the light came on, and I realized that the "craft" is teachable. The drive and passion for your product are not. However, enthusiasm is contagious if you spread the germ. The business of being in business is what takes companies with a great idea to the top. It would be best if you have a company structure, for without a framework, you can go down the rabbit hole. Once in that hole, you may never jump out and your doors might close forever, and quickly.

> **The "craft" is teachable. The drive and passion for your product are not.**

The light came on and I had to have a conversation with myself. "No matter how hard I work, or how good I am at what I do, will ever make up for the ignorance of how to run a company."

Here was the outcome of my conversation: Having street smarts is critical for operating an institution. It is a must to have someone on board to teach you the business of business. Understanding the financials, corporate structure, growth, and investment in the future must be your highest priority, even when you don't think you have time. If you perform this part of your operation, then you won't have much time left to do your craft. However, you must learn it and understand it to succeed and grow.

> **You have to be in the business of being in business.**

Since I am good at my craft, I chose to hire someone good at business. Rich, with a degree in business and finance, thought he was good at running the company. However, he had the degree, but not the management skills. It turned out that his wiring is for sales and marketing. We found a reputable coach that would come in monthly to not only read our financials but also teach me what the numbers meant, and how to read those financials myself.

As I learned to follow the statements for growth and stability, the advisor would increase my knowledge with forecasting. I was learning how to grow by reinvesting my capital. Having a strategy gave me a plan to follow.

I found that I am a great leader, but a horrible manager. People who could keep up and follow me learned to move up the ladder. I was so busy that I didn't even notice the other employees that were not showing up on time or underachieving. My brain could not comprehend why everyone would not work, whether he or she was on or off the clock. I could not understand why work was not constantly on everyone else's mind. After all, that was how I worked!

I had promoted sweet Irene to one of our account managers. She was a terrific administrator. Wow, she knew what the company did, how we did the work, and she worked until the job was completed. What more could you ask for in a manager?

Sweet Irene was sweet! She understood the employees' problems. Oh, they couldn't make it to work because their car broke down. Or once I heard her talking to an employee about their cat. "Well, of course I understand why you're not coming in. Cats don't just jump off the balcony and die every day. Oh no! He was trying to get to the bird cage that you put on the porch? I didn't know cats would actually try to get a bird out of the cage. My, well, do you really need four days off for that?"

My practice of promoting a hard worker to a manager was suddenly flawed. It takes someone with a natural ability to manage, to manage well. Setting limits comes naturally to this type of person.

My management style consisted of hiring everyone from my church because they were "Christians," and according to scripture they should "Work willingly at whatever you do, as though you were working for the Lord rather than for people." (Colossians 3:23)

There is also that thing about Jesus dying for us because we could never live up to all the laws and we are all flawed. In essence, I had to fire all my church people and find another church. We were ostracized and taken off the "A" list at church social functions. We had a new rule in the company:

Don't hire anyone from any church that we attend—now or in the future.

One of my favorites was Doreen the decorator. She had a talent for decorating and became a good friend. Her husband was a closet gay man who decided to do his reveal as their last daughter was going into high school. He left his wife for his new man. She was devastated and needed a job urgently; we hired her as my husband's assistant. Boy did his office look great! She had beautiful pictures on the wall, his desk and floor cleaned, and plants in exact locations to add greenery. Then the business chewed her up and spit her out. She was not wired to do what we expected and needed her to do. Rich doesn't have the gift of teaching. He left her on her own to "figure out" what needed to be done. Here was yet another friend down the drain after just six weeks.

One of our brightest failures was a young teen with a baby that I decided needed some nurturing as she matured into adulthood. She could quickly learn anything put before her. Rocking the job, she became the star player. That was if you didn't count all her absences. There was one excuse after another. We had to let her go. The company now developed another rule: You must show up for work!

> **Checking a body's pulse is not the way to hire anyone.**

Not much time went by until this young woman knocked at the door again, stating her personal problems were in the past. I welcomed her with open arms, excited to have her talents for our eager clients. I felt like a prodigal daughter came home. I said, "Get out the fatten lamb, prepare a feast, and give her a few great accounts for coming back." Within a few short months, we were back in the same situation again, where attendance was not consistent. I would love to tell you I learned my lesson, but I repeated this same mistake with the prodigal yet another time before I threw in the towel on my management skills.

When you create a business, there will be times that you need bodies. Your attitude may be, "anybody will do." During interviews, word bubbles will pop into your mind as you look at the candidate: *They are breathing. Coherent words are coming out of their mouth. Hmm, they have only had three jobs this year and have a reasonable explanation for leaving.* At this point, something spurts out of your mouth."OK, great, when can you start?"

Checking a body's pulse is not the way to hire anyone.

Taking vitals only was the case with Sandra, the squirrel lady. She stayed outside most of the day feeding squirrels instead of managing the finances. Sandra made such an impression on me that I would have dreams that haunted me. One night I woke up in a sweat because Sandra and her squirrel were in my bed.

We replaced Sandra the Squirrel Lady with Betty the Bedbug Lady. We felt sorry for her because she had sores on her arms and legs. She applied ointment to try to clear the lesions. Betty assured us that the condition was not contagious. Her open wounds turned out to be bedbug bites. Some of the critters tagged along on her clothes and into the office. Her tag-a-long friends ended in an office fumigation that lasted weeks. This also gave me nightmares.

> **Some people are creators and developers, some are managers, and some are lazy asses.**

It's also tempting to have a savior complex. Now that you own a business, you can "save the world" by giving employment to those in need. Formerly incarcerated for selling meth, Peppy Pricilla was fresh out of prison on work release. There it was—the opportunity to make a difference in society. Our company would rehabilitate her, plus teach her a skill to make a living. She wanted to take care of her family which would enable her to feed her children now that she was out of jail. All she needed was a break to get on her feet.

Pricilla's personal problems were very entertaining for the staff, and they were aired publicly—sometimes multiple times each day. Fighting with her boyfriend either on the phone or at our doorstep was as common as getting a cup of coffee. There was plenty of gossip for fuel, but no work being done to produce the fire that was needed.

Hiring family also doesn't work. Your Aunt Julie may be fun to shop with, but put her in the office and she might not be the sharpest crayon in the box. This happened when I hired an in-law to be an administrator. It didn't take long for that in-law to become an outlaw. With family, mending a relationship is like tearing down the Berlin Wall when things go south—and 99 percent of the time, they will go south.

Those were the workers that could never reach potential without being managed. My coach taught me how to examine skills so that each manager was right for the job, and the workers were wired for the job they performed. If they weren't talented, hiring them would not be possible.

Vampires came to work a few months after we settled into our new office. Yes, they are real, or at least they think they are. Victoria appeared so normal in our interview. Moreover, her résumé glowed with desirable skills in the automotive field. Our inability to connect with any of her past employers didn't seem to matter because in the auto industry, people move around a lot.

Victoria was very well-spoken, ordinary, but, attractive with long black hair, and possessed a go-getter attitude, or so I thought. But on her first day of work, she arrived in a low-cut, all black, long flowing dress, with her not so perky breasts sagging openly for all to see. I managed to mutter, "Oh, um, let me get you to our production manager to get you started." Quickly rushing Victoria past the men in the building, I ushered her into our production manager's office.

There she sat, smiling earnestly through blood-red lipstick that stuck to her white teeth. "I am so happy to be here. Being in Colorado is so exciting. I can't wait to get started. I have heard so much about all of you," she managed as Jami, our production manager, entered the room.

Jami gasped and took in so much air that she choked a bit, seeing Victoria for the first time. "Hhhhmmm," she said, clearing her throat. "Hi, Victoria, I'm Jami, nice to meet you. Now you need to run home, contain the girls, dress appropriately, and then you can come back." Both participants maintained smiles.

Victoria's happiness didn't waver one moment while she explained, "Oh, I'm a vampire, this is my religion, and how we dress. I know my rights. You can't persecute me for my beliefs. I am protected by law. I researched the California law and you cannot keep me from working due to my faith."

"Well, Victoria, this is Colorado, not California," Jami pointed out. "In Colorado, we believe in covering up your personal parts and our employees have the right not to view what should remain hidden. So if you want the job, cover the girls. Otherwise, you and the girls can find another employer." Jami held the door open while she spoke.

> **A direct approach means no one ever has to wonder where you stand.**

At that, our vampire disappeared in the sunshine, vanishing before our eyes, never to return. In her disappearance came a personal revelation that I spoke out loud: "That is what a good manager does! They are able to be firm, and direct. The employee will always know where they stand." I knew that what I needed do was to get out of my production manager's way and let her do what I paid her to do. Obviously, Jami had a firm hand on managing.

The next steps taught me how to plan organization charts. This became a puzzle, and the pieces slowly started to fit. I studied team management skills. By doing this I found answers to how many people could effectively manage a group. We invested in testing to make sure the right people had a natural ability for the job.

Some people are creator developers, some are managers, and some are lazy asses. There are those who work to live, and those who live to work. To own a business, you must be one that lives to work, be a creator, hire a manager, and get rid of the lazy asses. Don't try to save the world, keep family as family, and find the right people for the job.

**Lesson Learned:** An Indi car can take off and finish safely only if the driver is in control and doesn't over-correct the turns.

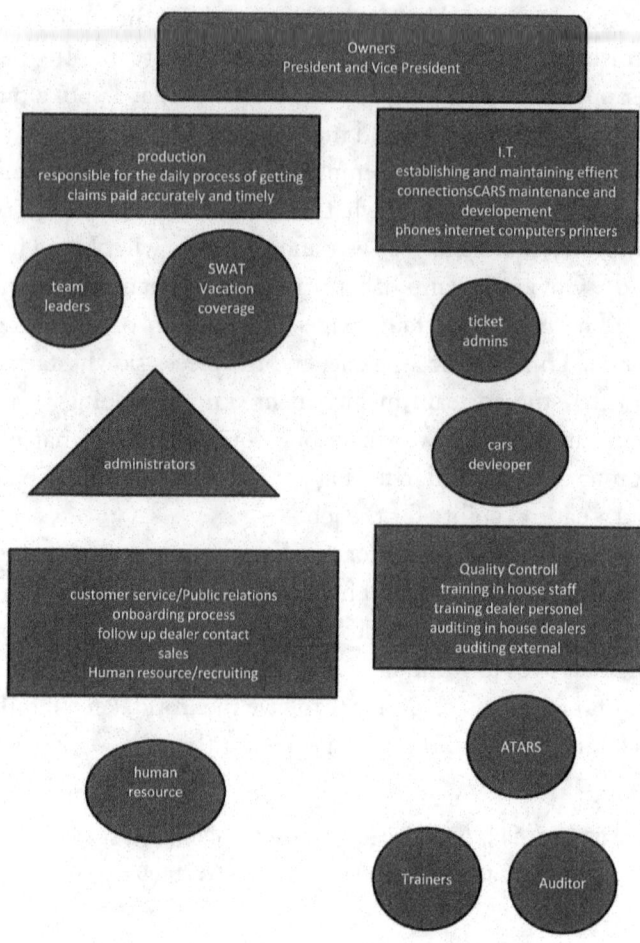

Example of our organizational chart in the beginning stages

# CHAPTER 10

# Creating a New Department

*"I had no idea that our road trip would be a
new road map for a new revenue stream."*

For two days after Victoria left, I didn't know where to go or what to do. Thinking, *Is this it? I'm done? I'll die with nothing to do.*

Rich still had plenty to do with sales on the rise, and I found myself jealous of his importance. His gracious invitation to tag along with him on a sales trip enticed me to believe, *This might be an opportunity for me to have something new to do.* We would take off for a road trip together.

A leading manufacturer was using our company to test

experimental vehicles using flight recorders to keep track of data as we traveled. We were assigned several luxury brands with radical engine changes hidden under the hood. There were two Jaguars with test engines and one Lincoln Continental that also had test equipment.

That Lincoln was put to the test in more than one way; it was animal-tested to the max. After moving the office out of our house, we moved to a small rural town in Colorado to save money. We had eight acres of land that had a big garden to grow our own food, along with livestock that we used for food also. Our two boys were into 4H, which kept them out of trouble most of the time. We had five horses, three pigs, two lambs, two goats, a potbelly pig, two ferrets, three dogs, several barn cats, and no partridge in a pear tree.

I came home one night after work and fed my lambs a bit of feed to entice them to come into their stalls. One started choking really badly, and I jumped in the stall, lifted his head, and started rubbing his throat. I felt the small grains inside his throat and tried pushing them down the passage. I told my lamb, "Come on, sweetie, or else I am going to place my fingers down your throat!"

I must admit I panicked, but my instinct kicked in and I quickly threw the lamb into the Lincoln Continental with its rich leather seats and sped off to the local vet. The vet said he had never seen anything like it in his life. That scared the daylights out of me because I thought he was going to tell me the lamb was going to die, but he quickly added, "Never seen a lamb in a Lincoln before."

The wooly creature stuck his head between the seats, looked at the vet, and let out a belch. We didn't tell the manufacturer about the animal testing; we figured they might not want that to go public. It could have attested to Ford's slogan, though—*Built Ford tough*.

> **The service department is similar to an Emergency Room at the hospital. Sick vehicles arrive, some with mystery ailments, many are urgent repairs, and a few arrive with emotional owners hanging onto the last shred of hope for their automobile.**

After the lamb's miraculous recovery, Rich and I took off for that sales adventure to Hobbs, New Mexico, leaving our miniature farm in our oldest boy's capable hands. We hit the open road in the Lincoln, heading south on Colorado's I-25.

Somewhere around Santa Fe, the road trip transformed our discussions with creative energy and a new idea began to emerge. Rich and I talked about how not all of our clients wanted to outsource processing; some dealers would always want to keep in-house administrators, and in some cases, it is better for them to do this. What was needed in the industry was training for those stores wanting to maintain control of administration in their own dealerships. Not just any training, either; the factory offers sterile training on perfect examples.

The service department, on the other hand, is similar to an Emergency Room at the hospital. Sick vehicles arrive, some with mystery ailments, many are urgent repairs, and a few arrive with emotional owners hanging onto the last shred of hope for their automobile. The service manager can be found ordering technicians to administer triage to critical vehicles. The whole department manages to put a Band-Aid on mechanical patients to keep traffic flowing. In the middle of all the confusion, critical policy and processes most often get tossed out the window.

Our training would consider the real-world scenarios that dealerships face daily. We wanted to teach staff how to stay compliant in the good, the bad, and the ugly hustle of the average service department. This was a program that no one offered anywhere in the automobile business.

> **In the middle of the confusion, critical policy and processes most often get tossed out the window.**

Rich and I excitedly brainstormed, naming our newly-designed product "Powertraining.© " I mapped flowcharts with sticky notes on side windows as Rich drove. The notes flowed over to the back glass. Applying square notes for absolutes and turning them sideway diagonally for exceptions, I scribbled each process. By the time we reached Roswell, we had a new product to sell and one we could charge $10,000 for. This was a time for celebration, and one I knew the aliens in Roswell could appreciate because our new idea was foreign to the automobile industry. We eagerly took in each hokey tourist museum in Roswell, laughing about the fake alien on display and enjoying the new success we would undertake with Powertraining© .

After our Roswell side trip, we hopped back in the car, and Rich began selling Powertraining© on his mobile phone. He wasn't shy when he explained our process, nor was he apologetic about the high-dollar price tag. By the time we reached our destination, we had three new clients and I had a new job to do—training, leaving managing to my manager. This added a new product to the revenue stream. Having only one product limits a company's ability for income and limits the capability for success in the long run. We needed to stay on the cutting edge of the industry.

Many times, you can look back to your childhood and see what prepared you for your success in running a company. Some memories that you once felt to be misfortunes could be the ones that helped you grow the most. Likewise, the wonderful remembrance is one that you cling to when managing.

> **"There is too much horse shit here, so there has to be a pony somewhere."**

Growing up in Shawnee, Oklahoma, I found myself on horseback most of the time, which taught me many valuable lessons about business.

One of my favorite sayings is, "There is too much horse shit here, so there has to be a pony somewhere." Business translation: don't forget why you are doing what you are doing.

Too often the workday is like shoveling poop, meaning we get so deep into the day-to-day grind, we are just trying to keep up. That is why a mission statement is so important. It keeps you focused on the pony that is creating the big pile of poop.

Remember that earlier I stated that I knew my craft, but I didn't know how to run a business? I strongly recommend that you set aside time to focus on operating the business, or hire a coach, counselor, or business friend that will make you sit down to think. What is your pony? Where is your pony? Most importantly of all, what is your pony's purpose? Then you can ride the pony in the direction that you need to go. This becomes your mission statement.

Once you have the mission statement accurately described, post it on your wall, share it with everyone, and read it daily. It sounds easy to do, right? NOT! Writing out your purpose, mission, and vision statement takes time. Don't rush this process. Rewrite the remarks a few times before you settle on the one you will stick to.

Each department should also have a mission, vision, and purpose statement. Finally, you can drill down to each person, assigning each a mission, vision, and purpose.

Now everyone knows why they are shoveling shit!

Stay focused on the core competencies, the reason that you are here. Own up to your failures. Constantly correct your course to stay on your mission.

---

**Lesson Learned:** For a race car driver, speed is the purpose and focus is on the track. The mission is to drive the car and win the race.

## 3. MISSION STATEMENT

### VISION

Our vision is to become and then sustain the position as the largest and standard for automotive warranty claims and service management company in North America.

### MISSION

Our mission is to deliver complete world class service to 2,200 dealers in North American by the end of 2022.

### PURPOSE

We are passionate about: 1) Removing the warranty processing stress off our customers; 2) Allowing personnel the opportunity to balance their lives and earn a good living by developing admirable skills; 3) Offer our employees the opportunity to advance in the company and enhance their quality of life by developing their God given skills; and 4) Give our owners a respectable return on investment.

Our mission statement

BUCKLE UP FOR BUSINESS SUCCESS

Before I could walk, Dad had me on horseback
to teach me about common horse sense

## CHAPTER 11

# Patience and Persistence

*"Patience is the ability to wait or continue doing something despite difficulties. ... Persistence is the ability to stick with the plan!"*

As hard as it is to hear, things happen at the right time, at the right place, in your life. Oh, I know you don't want to listen to any preaching, but God grants us blessings according to our ability, just like you as a parent give your children tasks according to what they are ready for. If you don't think your child has enough experience in a situation or has enough wisdom or discernment, then you restrict his or her progress until he or she is ready.

One example that comes to mind is when I had our teenage daughter fighting with me over the phone about wanting to buy push-up bras and thong panties. First of all, there was nothing much to push up yet, much less the appropriateness of her request. I remember clearly my humor as I spoke. "I tell you what, when you can flush the toilet and brush your teeth twice a day, then we can talk about a push-up bra and thongs. How about that?" I didn't realize that I had a crowd of mothers standing around me, listening to my side of the conversation. As I clicked the phone off, I could hear laughter and applause from a small group that gathered nearby. I could imagine other parents stealing my lines to use on their own teen at some time or another.

Our own self-confidence often exceeds our ability many times in life. That doesn't mean that you will never be able to wear a push-up bra, or whatever the desire you possess; patience just means that you're not ready for the item right now in your life.

> **Increasing your knowledge means doing your investigation, talking to others about it, and finally taking a chance on your decision.**

Our daughter was experiencing the difficult task of growing up and maneuvering through high school. I really can't think of anything more difficult in life than the peer pressure in those horrible teen years. She needed patience while the time passed, she matured, and she reached graduation. There were a lot of lessons she learned reaching that goal.

God does want to bless us in huge ways, but we have to be willing to put in the work to be able to grow. Growing is making mistakes while trying not to make too many of them. Increasing your knowledge means doing your investigation, talking to others about it, and finally taking a chance on your decision. This doesn't always mean that things will turn out for good.

Let's revisit my daughter, that same teenage girl at 16, for an example. She had been grounded from using the car due to some misbehavior. Here's my view when dealing with teenagers: the best leverage is the car and the wallet. If you have small children that will someday become teens, remember these wise words—wallet, car. Teens can't do much without those two items.

> **We have a part to play in every circumstance we are in, whether it is a success or a failure. To be successful, it is imperative that we see our own mistake in situations.**

The night in question, our teen increased her knowledge by investigating our movie times and how long we as parents would be away from the house. She phoned her friends, asking them their opinion about the length of the movie and did they think she would get caught if she took the car for a spin. Finally, she took a chance and drove to a friend's house, thinking we would not find out. She didn't count on the fact that the hood would be warm to the touch when we arrived home. This miscalculation delayed her progress in getting her wheels back even longer.

The same is true of us adults because we make some of these fundamental errors in our lives. To be successful, it is imperative that we see our own mistake in situations, even if it wasn't entirely our own doing. We have a part to play in every circumstance we are in, whether it is a success or a failure.

Our company now has what we call a "2X rule." Simply put, when you reach out to a person for information and there is no response; wait 24 hours and ask again. After waiting another 24 hours, your request must be moved up the ladder to the supervisor in line. That process continues until the request eventually moves up to the president of the company or until the information is received. Even though this is a simple rule, the process is the hardest for employees to remember.

Angry April struggled with this rule the most. Her receivable schedule of unpaid items was enormous month after month. We counseled April to better her performance.

Finally, at the last write-up April blurted out, "Well, you don't know how hard I have tried to get answers from the client, so I can get these claims paid! I emailed a hundred times, and no telling how many phone calls, but no one at the dealership answers me!"

Her supervisor had one question before handing Angry April her walking papers. "I have not seen any 2X requests for help from you to assist with your client." Angry April signed her termination and left with five words, "Oh, I forgot about that." April exhibited patience and persistence to the point of wearing out the company's patience with her.

I can give you one example where I used patience and persistence together and it paid off. In the early days of claims processing, we had to use mail to send in forms to receive payment. The manufacturer would either reject the claim or send back the paperwork to be corrected, or they would pay by check.

I diligently sent claims in weekly but after a couple of months had received no payment or rejections. I double-checked the address and confirmed I had been mailing the claims to the correct location. My impatience had me throwing a fit and trying to devise a way to get the manufacturer to pay me, but the payoff was because of my persistence.

The next batch of weekly claims I mailed in had a chocolate bar inside. A big chocolate bar. Within a week, I received a check from the claims processor for $10,000!

Wow, I bought a case of chocolate and continued including treats in each package I mailed.

> **Many business dealings that might have you feeling impatient need time to breathe before you make a choice you will be sorry for.**

For the most part, entrepreneurs are an impatient bunch. To build a successful business, you have to hustle and be somewhat of a hard-charger. Impatience, unsurprisingly, is a common byproduct of the entrepreneurial mindset.

I want to talk about one other virtue before ending the chapter. Patience and persistence have a friend called Breath. Breath vs. Breathe. Breathe is a verb we use for the process of inhaling and exhaling. Breath is a noun that refers to a full cycle of breathing. It can also refer to the air that is inhaled or exhaled.

Sometimes the interruptions in our lives are breaths. They give us time to think about our choices, our circumstances, and let us ponder the next move.

Breath can keep you out of trouble. Many business dealings that might have you feeling impatient need time to breathe before you make a choice you will be sorry for.

At the end of his career, our business advisor sent me a nasty email that upset me greatly. My immediate impatient response was to fire back a reply full of bitterness and right-fighting. Instead, I called on my friend, Breath, for help. I decided to open the email and let the subject breathe overnight. The result—the advisor, realizing his mistake, had an apology in my inbox the next morning. Boy, was I glad I had not sent an ugly response.

The best we can do is to still use the three principles from above—do your homework, talk with others you trust, and take a chance.

If you never take a chance, then you can never succeed.

---

**Lesson Learned:** Excellent race drivers use their good judgment to avoid situations in which they might need to use their skills.

# CHAPTER 12

# Honesty is the Best Policy

*"Honesty sounded so easy until
I looked up the meaning."*

Integrity is hard, and I genuinely believe that someone needs to be behind you nudging, "Just tell the truth, it will be OK." It's easy to visualize the depiction of an angel hovering on your right shoulder, whispering, "Honesty is the best policy." On your left shoulder sits the devil, shouting loudly, "Make an excuse and a little dishonesty will make it not look so bad. It's a white lie, and they don't count, ya know." A bald-faced lie will always be found out, but a small story concerning the circumstances will allow the indiscretion to be palatable. At least, that's how the story used to go for me.

Rich has always been proud of the fact that he doesn't lie. He will remind everyone in attendance, "I don't lie. I will never lie to you." I know this is mostly true, except when he leaves out crucial information. This affirms that we all struggle and fall short. There is a Bible verse about that, too, because not one of us has escaped the temptation of telling a falsehood. With all this evidence, Rich still insists he doesn't lie, which is a lie. But he is the one that stands steadfastly beside me when the devil is yelling in my ear to claim something other than the truth.

Number one on our new company's strategic imperatives is, "Own up to our failures and make the required changes." I wrote that statement because it is the most important quality we can offer to our clients and employees. Dang if it hasn't bit me in the butt a million times. Owning your own failure does get easier the more you practice it. I sure wish that I had a talent for owning up to mistakes, so I didn't have to practice as much.

The hardest admission of failure came at a high price of $16,000 on a mistake I personally made.

Jake, a long-time client, friend, and person I admire, trusted me to assemble a list of claims not paid by the manufacturer that were too old to process due to a computer glitch. Jake came from old money—meaning money had been passed down. His dealership had been in his family for many generations. He dressed impeccably—thousand-dollar suits and round glasses—yet you never felt upstaged around him. Jake was business, but never in the cold atmosphere of "It's just business." Loyalty he honored, expected, and freely administered back to those around him.

I carefully listed each claim number, dollar amount, and date in an Excel spreadsheet. My data was extracted from a receivable schedule provided by Jake's staff. With confidence, Jake turned the sheet over to the manufacturer for payment, and it was approved. The disturbing phone call came from the receivable clerk in his dealership's office: "Lisa, I think you left off some claims. I'm seeing around $16,000 overage that you don't have on your spreadsheet."

*That cannot be right*, I thought. *I worked hard on it. I'm not that stupid.* But I went back to check and, sure enough, $16,000 was the figure that was not accounted for and therefore not approved to be paid. My heart sank, and immediately, my brain started conjuring up excuses, lies, how to cover it up. Could I enter the claims with fictitious dates so they would pay without approval? They would indeed fly right through. No one would ever know, would they? The little angel was nowhere present, just the devil quipping in my ear. That night there was no drifting off to sleep. Dollar bills floated under my eyelids and I counted them to $16,000, with not one ounce of slumber.

Morning finally came with the sun shining, bringing pleasant warmth to everyone on the earth except me. My heart stored doom and gloom while we drove to the dealership, where Jake awaited our arrival. Rich, forever my chauffeur and my support, parked in front of the dealership. The building itself was intimidating—huge doors led to the showroom of marble tile that held expensive luxury vehicles polished to a high gloss, inviting a new customer to purchase them. We proceeded upstairs to the offices, passing a gym with more equipment than a membership club owns. My bladder protested, not from the amounts of liquid consumed, but from the nervousness that caused it to quiver, making me duck into the bathroom before getting to Jake's office.

Opening the solid wood door, I was met with more opulence. Black onyx toilets and sinks stared at me, reminding me of Jake's money I had thrown down the toilet. I was about to tell this man to flush $16,000 down one of these beautiful commodes, and I felt sick for mishandling his money. It was money he had worked for, his dad had worked for, and his grandfather had earned. How could I have been so reckless?

> **You will always know that you made the right choice if you are honest.**

Jake quickly stood to greet us when we entered his office. He purposely walked to the front of his desk to shake my cold hand as he put the other warm hand on my shoulder. I couldn't help but take in the personal effects of his office, noting pictures of his smiling family and golf memorabilia.

Tears kept threatening to leak from my eyes, but I willed them back so I could confess my sins without hesitating. Jake listened without interruption and then stared at me sitting there with my head bowed and my hands folded to constrain the trembling. Dang it, why didn't he say something?

Jake looked out his office windows, pondering his next statement, and then finally spoke. "Hmm, before we go off the deep end here, let's get those claims added to your spreadsheet this morning. I will call the manufacturer to explain what happened, because it is an honest oversight. Then together we will ask them to add these to the exception onetime payment. After we get their answer, we can worry about what comes next. I believe that those who don't ask, don't get. The answer may be yes, in which case we have no need for alarm. If the answer is no, then we will work out a repayment solution, but we may not even need that conversation."

The dam burst, and there was nothing I could do to prevent a flood that ran over the hills of my cheeks. Jack saw a humble spirit that needed compassion. When he rose to escort us out of the office, he continued his mentorship. "Get on out there and add those numbers. I'll meet you back here after lunch, and we'll make that call."

The numbers were added, the call was made, and the claims were paid. Honesty paid off. If it had not, the $16,000 repayment would have been a hard pill to swallow. The important lesson was that I was at peace no matter which way the decision went. That is where you need to come to in business. Do the right thing, no matter what. There will be some losses and some wins. You will always know that you made the right choice if you are honest.

**Lesson Learned:** In racing, integrity is telling myself the truth about my performance; honesty is admitting the truth to other people.

# CHAPTER 13

# Adventure

*"Adventure is an unusual and exciting, typically hazardous experience or activity, especially the exploration of unknown territory."*

There will be times in your business where you will need to sacrifice almost everything to achieve your goals. Taking chances, gambling on the future and calculated risks are part of the entrepreneur spirit. Everyone would own a business if it were easy. Only the brave will have the tenacity to complete the task and hold on for the ride. An exciting trip on a roller coaster has fewer ups and downs than owning a business. It's called being all in. Most of the time, being all in is not comfortable nor pleasant.

The years from 2004 to 2006 were fantastic for vehicle sales. Our new company depended on the car sales because with the new automobile came a factory warranty for at least three years or 36,000 miles. Automotive Warranty Network (AWN) was the go-between for the dealership and the manufacturer. Dealerships could choose to outsource the billing process to our administrators, and we received payment on a percentage of dollars collected.

With the addition of our Powertraining© service, we captured the entire market in factory warranty service. The training offered an alternative to dealerships that did not want to outsource collections. AWN could now go to the service department and train its staff to do the same process. Our services encompassed teaching the administrator, technicians, service advisors, and managers to collect factory dollars and stay compliant with all the laws and policies the manufacturer enforced. The price tag was only $10,000 – $12,000 for the week, plus expenses. Those dollars were pure gravy to the bottom line, added to the number that our administrators were bringing in for outsourced processing.

Rich and I were the only trainers, so we found ourselves on the road 48 out of 52 weeks during those years. The first trip was the hardest, as we had no money to start the process. We needed that first paycheck to start the ball rolling so we would have money to travel. Our first trip was memorable, painful, enjoyable, horrible, and wonderful all at the same time. Rich pulled money from our personal account for airline tickets, leaving our house payment overdue by 30days.

The flight to Los Angeles International Airport (LAX) to train in a luxury auto group was scheduled, and we were on our way. We were about to see our plan come to life; we felt like Dr. Frankenstein as his monster took its first breath.

Once in LAX, we could not rent a vehicle because our credit card had just enough room on it for a hotel for the week. Our pockets held a meager amount of cash that could allow us to eat if we budgeted appropriately. The Super Shuttle ride at $16 was the only transportation in our price range to take us to the Quality Inn, which incidentally was not a quality accommodation in the least.

> **"Ha, the speed limit is not for expert drivers like me."**

We took our seat in the last of four rows on the bus. The dark-skinned driver spoke broken English with a hint of Arabic. "Welcome, put your seatbelts on please we take off now." Before the last word left his lips, his foot slammed onto the accelerator, throwing all passengers into the back of their seat cushions with stunned expressions.

The blue van wove in and out of lanes in LA traffic with intermittent hard braking that propelled passengers forward. Once off the highway, we proceeded to the first drop-off via a narrow, winding avenue at high speed. One man spoke up. "Excuse me, sir. Excuse me, but the speed limit is only 25 miles per hour here." As he spoke, he held tightly to the back of his seat to prevent tumbling to the floorboards.

"Ha, the speed limit is not for expert drivers like me. Oh no, my friend, I am an excellent driver." Our bearded, dark-skinned coachman laughed, showing his perfect white teeth through his whiskers. "Do not try this at home, my friend, for you could not make it." The bus hit a bump at that moment, sending Rich's and my heads into the padded roof of the vehicle, our seat cushions bouncing underneath us.

My own words came out mixed with laughter, as I held tightly to the back of the seat in front of me. "My husband always wanted to drive like this with me in the car."

This time our escort turned his head to address me in the back seat. We could see his full red turban. "Ha, is fun, yes? Tell your husband to learn, yes?" Truly the driver was enjoying the ride as much as I was, but others in the middle seats could view the road ahead in horror as each curve approached.

Rich and I were one of the last to disembark. Still feeling exhilarated, we tipped the driver a generous five dollars that would mean we would share a taco instead of each having a whole tortilla to indulge in; however, it was worth the adventure. Our new comrade flashed one last smile our way as we exited. "Goodbye, my friend, until our paths cross again."

After removing yet another germ-infested striped bedspread, Rich and I fell into our inferior bed at the Quality

Inn, still exuberant from our motor ride. I did pull back the fitted sheet to check for bedbugs and thankfully found none. Never mind we were hungry—there was a free breakfast in the morning, and we would fill our belly and take bananas for a snack after we got a good night's sleep.

The next day we were picked up and greeted with enthusiasm by the service manager of the luxury dealer group. Rich worked with service management, implementing a new process, as I worked in the shop with technicians, perfecting write-up procedures as they made repairs on the vehicles. By Friday, there was a harmonic orchestra in tune between management, the technicians, and administration. We gathered with all personnel at the conference table for an exit meeting where we were praised for our product and service and given a $12,000 check for the plane trip home, where it would quickly enter our dwindled bank account.

> **If you go into business, be ready to hang on for the ride.**

Powertraining© was a success, and word spread at the speed of a forest fire through the dealership communities that this program would improve cash flow and communications in the warranty repair process. One particularly gracious endorsement glowed, "AWN saw the potential in our staff. They pushed our employees up to success, not down to despair." Rich and I left our office in the capable hands of our managers and staff as we brought the gravy train dollars back to deposit into the bank. New clients poured in, with the company riding a wave of prosperity. The money financed new growth without borrowing a dime to create debt.

Little did we know that troubled times lay ahead. Like any surfer can tell you, all waves eventually peter out, and your surfboard sinks into the ocean. Our wave was about to run out.

**Lesson Learned:** Race drivers have to trust their vehicle and their skills, but keep their seatbelt fastened for safety in the adventure of the race.

## BUCKLE UP FOR BUSINESS SUCCESS

In the stores Powertraining. ©

## CHAPTER 14

# Keep Moving, No Matter What

*"Mom, keep 'r movin, no matter what just keep 'r movin."*

— *A quote from Maddie*

For anyone feeling desperate in business, this chapter is for you. If you are going into business for yourself, then you will face times where it appears there is no way out. You probably will experience that feeling more than once.

The addition of Powertraining© allowed our new company to improve and grow. We were able to finance our growth by adding staff slightly before they were needed, giving employees the chance to be appropriately trained before taking on a client. Our customer satisfaction index was off the chart, causing our patrons to recommend our services to their peers daily. Working was fun. The busier it was, the higher we flew, and the higher we soared, the better the job we did.

The ringing in of the 2008 New Year's bell broke our high-flying financial bubble. The downfall in the market led to total silence from our customers, who were fighting to hold onto their wallets. New car sales weakened due to the high fuel prices and economic downturn. Toyota sales dropped 33.9 percent and had a $1.7 billion loss. Japan slashed vehicle production and the American Big Three were in trouble. While the government rushed in to rescue General Motors and Chrysler, Ford secured a line of credit due to the lack of sales.

The trickledown effect to the dealerships was more of a tsunami as stores cut staff and extras to keep the doors open. Many long-standing companies boarded up and liquidated inventory. One of our clients made the headlines as their vehicles were loaded into trucks and the place vacated overnight.

Powertraining© was a luxury that was no longer affordable. Outsourcing for the excellent job of our administrators was replaced in-house by hourly clerks that could push the paper through to the manufacturer, who was no longer looking at the quality of the documents. The manufacturer and the dealership held onto whatever revenue they could muster.

> **Our bickering could be turned into a useful, spirited conversation.**

Many car establishments have family ownership, and their concern about holding on and taking care of their employees was paramount. Employees and customers were their neighbors and considered their people, inside their circle. Our company, AWN, was not in their circle; in fact, we were far outside their circle and not their people. We were in for trouble.

Within a few months, we were running out of money and chose to spend some of the little we had on a reputable consultant to help us bail water out of our ship and plug the holes. He was a tremendous help in making our management team work together to solve problems. We learned to listen to each other's creativity. One colossal takeaway was that our bickering could be turned into a useful, spirited conversation. We focused on the business at high volume without attacking one another personally, and that is okay when boundaries are set.

Our consultant looked at financials and taught us the term "low-hanging fruit": doing the easiest work first for the highest results. The term also had another meaning—to have us work to our strengths. In our case, we needed to pick low fruit from two trees to stay afloat. God equipped Rich with the natural ability to sell snow to people in Alaska, so his fruit would be mining dealers that were in trouble with receivables. My fruit was that I was able to process claims quickly and efficiently for dealers that were unable to collect money they were due from the manufacturer.

Now that the service departments chose to use untrained, inexperienced clerical help to collect warranty dollars, some were feeling the economic effects of high dollar repairs left uncollected. Rich had a perfect pitch, promising our company's expertise was not only needed but by only charging a small percentage of collections, the dealership would make 96 percent more money. One hundred percent of the claim was unpaid; if we collected 100 percent and charged 4 percent then you, Mr. Service Manager, are ahead by 96 percent.

Rich's wiring also comes with a natural personality trait that never allows the potential client to know you're desperate. He developed relationships that showed we wanted the dealer to get 96 percent, adding, "You can't afford not to use us because we don't cost a dime."

The rest of the management team was assigned to the other trees: picking out the people who were less valuable to the company—not personally, but in ability and production. These were people we could do without, either because we didn't need their functions anymore, or their duties could be assigned to someone else. Wow, this was an eye-opener! Our small company had become bloated with redundancies, which had me wondering, *How in the world did this happen right before my eyes?*

We quickly designated the survivors and the casualties, and began the awful process of letting people go, firing them, laying them off…in reality, there is no kind language to use. The bottom line is that someone is not going to have money to feed their family. I had pain in my heart for their welfare.

The woman who answered the phone, opened the mail, and cleaned the kitchen was the first to go. Following her were underachieving administrators whose work could feed another more qualified administrator. The first moral debate with our team quickly subsided when we were able to see the sacrificial lambs adopted by other businesses. In most cases, they bettered themselves, enabling our wounds to heal more quickly.

Our company seemed stable for a bit, but within a few months, our ship started taking on water again. Dealerships were not selling new vehicles. Without new sales, there was no warranty to have repairs and without the repairs, we had no job. Our team was down to core personnel.

> **How many times are you willing to lose before you win?**

The consultant couldn't bear to charge us money as he sat at our square dinner table, which substituted as a conference table. He informed our small band, "AWN is not going to make it. There is no way out, no miracle that will pull you into the black."

Rich was furious and slammed his fist onto the table. "You get out! No one, no one, says that to me! We will make it! If you believe you won't make it, then you won't. You can only win if you believe you can. Get out!"

Red-faced silence filled the room as the consultant quietly folded his financial book and walked to the door, the loud clacking of his shoes filling the dead space until he was outside the office. How are we going to make it? This was the question on my mind, but I knew not to let words to that effect leave my lips. Slowly, the others gingerly pushed back chairs, the sound vibrating in the room like a thunderstorm.

Only Rich and I were left at the table, not sure who would return tomorrow after hearing the prognosis for the company. Who could blame them if they found greener pastures?

I couldn't help wondering, *how many times can we lose before we win?* This time felt different than all the other times the company had been in trouble. With this loss, I was deflated, out of gas, and felt like I couldn't muster the energy to keep going until I remembered my daughter's words, "Mom, just keep 'r movin, no matter what."

. . . . . . . . . . . . . . . . . . . . . . . . . . . . . . . . . . . . . . . . . . .

**Lesson Learned:** A professional driver knows that a vehicle will perform a little over gross weight, but it won't go at all without fuel.

# CHAPTER 15

# Intimidation

*"Look people straight in the eye;
let them know you see them."*

Some people win by intimidating others. Then others let mere mortals bully themselves. In between, there is a space where we should find a plateau of commonality. There is a place to work without fear; fear lies to us. Those lies keep us from reaching heights we have the destiny to obtain. Fear paralyzes us and keeps our spirit hidden. The critical place to operate within is that neutral space when you are creating or managing your business.

I witnessed my Dad use neutral space on several occasions, which taught me to defuse heated situations in my business life. Working as the zone manager for Chrysler gave him the appearance of power, which he never leveraged as intimidation. The Chrysler building was equipped with security glass and locked to prevent outsiders from entering. The security prevented customers from walking into the zone building to yell at the executives about problems with their vehicles. There was a 1-800 number set up by the manufacturer for yelling, or complaints.

One unsatisfied customer who happened to be a 300-pound linebacker visited the zone headquarters demanding to see a high-ranking manager in the organization. I got to see Dad in action as the muscular football player angrily stood over him, unhappy with his vehicle experience. Dad didn't stand behind the glass or the locked door. He exited the security with a smile on his face and looked directly into the giant's eyes. The first words out of Dad's mouth threw water on the lit fuse. "Well, I don't know who in their right mind had the nerve to make you mad! That guy must have been crazy. Let's hear what the problem is with your vehicle."

> **You can offset these people by easing yourself into a position of equal power without them realizing what just happened.**

The statement, delivered with a smile, brought the man and the situation to a neutral space where the two men could talk to find a solution.

There are also those who use intimidation to put themselves in a position of power and strength. You can offset these people by easing yourself into a place of equal power without them realizing what just happened. There is magic and order to the craft of putting people at ease.

- *Use your smile-but only bring a genuine one*
- *Position yourself to even posture—for example, if they are standing, stand*
- *Acknowledge their problem*
- *Offer water or sustenance—bring the exact same for yourself*
- *Bring your ears to the party because you need to tell them you are there to listen*
- *Don't promise results but promise to do your best and then do your best*

I remember back to my first encounter with the Italian Stallion. He was a dealer owner from Malta, with a thick accent. Picture the Godfather on a yacht sailing the world with all his riches. The Italian Stallion maintained his office behind locked doors—to keep out anyone wanting to kill him, I presume. Once I was announced and let into Mr. Stallion's domain, I stepped onto the pure white carpet. Mr.

Stallion's desk sat high on a platform, and I ascended the steps to access his throne.

The Italian motioned me to sit at a chair slightly lower than his platform. Even though I was taken aback at the scene correctly set for intimidation, I smiled to show my delight to see him. Next, I moved the chair to his level so I could sit in front of his desk and talk to him. I wanted to be on his level. Moving the chair closer allowed me to be close to his stature. His back straightened a bit as he leaned back. Mr. Stallion's chin then tilted downward, and his eyes peered at me and my bold move.

Bringing my ears to the party, I said, "Let me hear what problems you are having and see if I have any ideas about how I can help." I dug into my bag to find a pen and paper. Sitting attentively, I had my hand steadied to jot down notes as he spoke.

The Italian poured his problems into my ears as I quietly listened. Only after he was empty did I ask questions that I had been jotting down. I told him, "I need a little more information in these certain areas."

I had warmth in my voice as I explained I would always perform my duties with his best interest in mind, but I would be honest and make decisions based on my "do the right thing" values.

The Italian stood up and shook my hand from behind his desk and proudly announced, "This, this is my girl."

Fear and intimidation can keep you from obtaining new business. This encounter taught me early on not to let the fear of intimidation stop my tenacity. The massive dealerships with the beautifully designed buildings had problems just as the small independent dealerships did; most often, on a larger scale. Never let fear, that liar, keep you from asking a client if they need your help.

> **Don't keep looking at the closed door; go on and open it.**

Let's go back to when I first met Jake with the large dealerships—my nearly $16,000 mistake. At the beginning of our relationship, I never in a million years thought someone like that would need little ole me to help him. I asked him for a receivable schedule that would show me how much the factory owed him. Usually, these schedules are at most 50 pages long, but when Jake's office manager printed his receivable schedule, she warned me it could take a while. It took most of the day—after printing, the stack of paper was at least two feet high Jake needed our company, and we were happy to help him get all that money.

Don't keep looking at the closed door; go on and open it.

---

**Lesson Learned:** Racecar drivers are always scared when they drive the first lap of their career.

## CHAPTER 16

# FHB

*"Feed your employees first."*

After our consultant left and we slimmed down to only essential employees, it was time to get back to the hard business of doing business. When a catastrophe happens to your company, there is a moment where you suck it up, put a smile on your face, and get back into the pool, so to speak.

I held my breath to see which core employees would show up after they witnessed Rich's anger. To my relief, all essential employees filed in the office doors right on time; in fact, some were quite early. Most managers already had their lists completed for who in their departments would be laid off, where the work would go, and how much could be added to whose plates to keep the company running. By the end of the day, we determined more people who were non-essential employees. This last group was given their walking papers, and business took on a new normal to bring revenue in the door.

> **Keeping an employee that isn't working out is the worst thing in the world that you can do for them.**

One of the hardest things to do is to lay people off or let them go for any reason. I have learned that keeping an employee that isn't working out is the worst thing in the world that you can do for them. Once you can understand that principle, you can let them go in love, because for them to stay in an unhealthy relationship will only continue to harm them. The employee will still be upset, still not like you, and you won't be their best friend. Reality is that they won't starve, and there is a good chance they won't end up homeless. But you still can't help feeling like a devil when you sever the relationship.

Once we took stock of the workloads and workforce, Rich and I took on every job that was left over that wasn't accounted for, along with the burden of accounting and sales. Our own paychecks stopped. This meant that our mortgage would be behind, the car was sold, peanut butter and jelly was on the menu, and other sacrifices were put into play. When you start or own a business, broken and hungry times will be on your menu. In fact, not just one time but too often will you find yourselves without necessities.

I had a small inheritance that was locked into a few certificates of deposit from my mother's death. It was heartbreaking to cash them in with a huge penalty, knowing that my mom would have wanted the money to go to better use. I hoped she wasn't watching from somewhere above to see the mess I made. I can never erase the emotions that day I withdrew the cash. Anger, yep, that was the first to rise. The humiliation I felt being in this position of failure again was overwhelming. Embarrassment—I did not want anyone in my family to find out Lisa messed up yet another time. I also was left with confusion—should I even keep trying to keep this company? Why not give up at this point?

With Rich hell-bent on keeping going and his never give up attitude; I decided I must keep moving toward the goal, no matter where the goal moved. The money would keep us afloat, pay necessary bills, and cover employee paychecks for the next several months if we were strictly using it for essential items.

Often our family didn't get a paycheck, and that included our grown children who were working for us at the time. We devised a new term that we often used in the office that no one else knew the meaning of: FHB. This stood for "family hold back." FHB came from the same term we used at the dinner table when I was growing up. If we had company and there wasn't enough food to go around, my parents would whisper, "FHB" and our family knew to take small portions. I can still picture my mom's face at the table; her smile never wavered when she passed the chicken plate my way. The sideways whisper as I was about to take a chicken fried breast, "FHB." I smiled too and passed the plate to our company and explained, "I just want some potatoes today, and some gravy."

When there was not enough to go around, our employees were fed first, and we took small or no portions to make sure we took care of the ones doing the work.

> **There will be family drama if you have a business, but you must keep working.**

This was the period that Rich's drinking began to spiral out of control. No one, not even I, knew the extent of his abuse. He had angry outbursts ending with his fist banging into desks to express his views. He would forget to return client phone calls when we needed the work desperately.

I believed that God did place a seed in our hand with the company. We planted it, watered it, pruned it, and fertilized it. Now the fruitful plant was trampled as if hail destroyed the greenery. I was not open to receiving Rich's advice, and he was not open to mine. The company was in a tug of war with only two people on the rope. Luckily, the rest of the team let go of the rope to tend to the company.

Life was dark, desperate, and lonely. We were both poor in spirit and materials, yet we kept working with all our might. The song lyrics played over in my head, "The darkest hour is just before dawn." How long until dawn?

There will be family drama if you have a business, but you must keep working. Problems will flood your personal life, which is no excuse for giving up. Bad things happen. Tough. Get in there and fight.

---

**Lesson Learned:** The racetrack and conditions are always subject to change. The driver knows that no matter what happens, drive the car.

# CHAPTER 17

# Perspective

*"Some horses just need to be put out to pasture or sent to the glue factory. Know when to cut your losses and move on."*

Don't get too comfortable in the saddle; a horse can spook at any time, tossing you right off its back. Business translation: don't get too comfortable behind your desk, or you might find yourself on the street.

Don't ride your horse hard and put it away wet. Horses that are ridden hard, work up a tremendous lather of sweat. If you don't cool them off and brush them down properly, they can get chills and muscle stiffness. These horses frequently become bad-tempered. Your employees should work hard, that's why you're in business, but you have to take care of them or they will become bad-tempered and leave you, or worse, they'll stay and make you and everyone else around them miserable.

Our company pays employees a fair wage, but our firm commitment to longevity is in our benefits. There are also small tidbits we provide at little cost to the company that pays off big for morale.

> **Small tidbits to encourage employees at little cost to the company can pay off big for morale.**

Offer affordable health care (if there is such a thing nowadays). Cut back a bit on salary to provide employees a way to stay healthy. Having a health savings account (HSA) can be a significant benefit. It allows employees to have a lower-cost medical plan with a savings account that builds over time to pay out-of-pocket deductibles. In the long run, the lower premium gives ample opportunity to save for the one yearly deductible if needed. These plans usually pay 100 percent of well-checks.

We bank (set aside) two days a year of paid time for every year worked for major illnesses. These days can't account for regular sick time. The extra days off are only for major surgery, cancer treatments, or life-changing disabilities.

I'll take a minute to tell you about Connie's experience

using these banked days. Connie developed breast cancer, and her surgery and treatment kept her out of work longer than her vacation and sick time combined. The company had banked ten extra days of major illness time for her five years of service. Not only did that help, but we had an employee offer to do her work on overtime, stating, "This is my donation to her, and I refuse a paycheck for the time I spend helping her. I am from a military family, and we leave no man behind."

Wow, just let that word get out in the company, and you've created a strong backbone in your workforce.

Another small way to encourage employees can be free or at little cost. We collect airline miles, hotel rewards, credit card rewards, and heck, even free restaurant rewards to dole out to employees when a job is well done. A free weekend on hotel points offers a well-needed retreat for an employee. A gift card for dinner and a movie can be much-needed date nights that will help employees escape the long hours they have put in. Spa and massage gifts take away the tension of a hard month end closing. These surprise cards encourage hard workers to work even harder for your company.

> **There is a careful balance to keeping employees happy but not spoiling them. I look at it as green, ripe, or rotten.**

One holiday season, we celebrated the 12 days of Christmas, giving each employee a small gift daily. This created excitement to come to work, wondering what the surprise was for the day. We got donations for coffee mugs, candy, hot chocolate, and socks from the dollar store, water bottles, and other small items. It was like a grown-up Elf on a Shelf for 12 days. Our morale was through the roof, and we finished the year with a robust bottom line.

There is a careful balance to keeping employees happy but not spoiling them. I look at it as green, ripe, or rotten. The green employees are growing and learning so as they learn you pay them a little more and then a little more. It's easy to gush on and on about the foliage they are producing. Every little thing you do for them can be compared to giving your plants Miracle-Gro; before you know it, that small plant has blossomed into a beautiful bush and has ripe fruit. The employee that reaches this stage is at full potential, and you think you have a winner.

Just like you can give a plant too much fertilizer at once or maybe too often, this can happen with an employee and in a short window that fruit can go from ripe to rotten. These moments have me scratching my head in bewilderment but, in reality, it is just human nature. Giving a child too many toys leaves him or her spoiled and wanting more.

Pay a fair wage. It is OK to pay the employee that works harder more than one who doesn't work hard. That is business. Probably the one not working so hard wouldn't be missed that much anyway. But be careful not to overpay for work that is expected to be done and is part of the job.

Make employees feel part of the company. If they are helping you meet goals, solve problems, and contribute to the growth of the organization, let them know it. Praise is as good as an extra buck.

Finally, don't keep an employee that breaks an absolute. It's easy to think, *That employee is great at their job, clients love them, and I can't lose them.* The truth is, you can't afford to keep them. When you save an employee that breaks an absolute in your core values, you are showing all your employees that your company values have no meaning.

> **When you keep an employee that breaks an absolute in your company core values, you are showing all your employees that your company values have no meaning.**

Lorna was one of our best administrators. I had complete trust and faith that the job she did would always be pretty much perfect but, mainly, I knew that Lorna would never break a core value.

The most critical value statement we have is never to change facts in a document. The mileage should never be altered to make a vehicle under warranty. Sometimes the claim has timed out due to the date, and it is never acceptable to change the repair date no matter what the reasoning. A certified technician must do certain repairs—changing a technician number to that of a certified technician while a non-certified tech did the work is considered fraud. That is like having a podiatrist performing heart surgery in a hospital.

Jake, the long-term client we talked about earlier, was going through a factory audit to make sure all claims paid throughout the year were complete and accurate. Since Lorna was the administrator on his account, I knew there would be no issues with his documentation or paperwork. I attended the meeting in full confidence and almost smugness, knowing we would get a glowing review.

A manufacturer pays the dealership for work performed to a vehicle while under factory warranty. When the audit team looks at documentation every few years, they look to see that all policies and laws were obeyed. Any paperwork that has even the smallest deviation from that policy will be charged back by the factory. The dealership will have to pay back the money for that repair.

The audit team passed out a report that broke down the chargeback dollars and the reasons for them.

Fraud due to altered documentation was the top offender, and a high-dollar figure flashed as if it were in neon lights, jumping off the page. I couldn't believe it. Bile came up in my throat, and I insisted on knowing the reason we were being accused of fraud. I knew that the dealership had to have done something because Lorna would never commit fraud.

Paperwork was passed to everyone at the table, showing a technician number was changed from a non-certified number to one that was certified. I was horrified, but just knew it had to be a typographical mistake. They passed around paper number two with the same issue. Then document number three and more followed, dropping one at a time for effect. The violent noise of paper hitting the table rattled like a grenade in my head, each setting off an explosion of embarrassment and anger.

Jake trusted me with his money. I trusted Lorna with Jake's money. The chargeback was about more than money, however; this was about integrity. Tarnishing Jake's name fell directly on my shoulders. I looked at him in his beautiful suit, which seemed to wrinkle before me. We were in the office that his grandfather helped build, then his father, and now him. My company's mistakes were desecrating the hallowed room.

> **Firing Lorna showed the compliant employees that their adherence to the company values was respected and honored.**

Jake had developed Parkinson's disease over the last few years. The stress of the audit allowed the disease to go full rampage, and he quietly held the offending arm down with his other steady hand. I wanted to reach out and hold his hand for him, but both of my hands shook worse than his.

I would have fired me right then on the spot, and I said as much to the audit team and Jake. "Our company never condones changing a document, and this is especially true for Jake's account. He is not only the client that we have the highest regard for, but he is a man I have always looked up to and respected. For this to happen on my watch is devastating. There is no excuse for the mismanagement, and I have extreme regret we have let him down. Jake's audit is our company's worst moment. Keeping with our values, we have no choice but to terminate Lorna. We also know this may very well be the end of our relationship. However, if allowed to remain, I can promise you that I will personally check your paperwork for documentation in the future."

My team and I humbly acknowledging our mistake was what everyone sitting at the table needed to hear. The debt was suspended for the time being, pending a review. Now our company needed to prove that we could walk the talk of integrity. Keeping Lorna as an employee was not an option for several reasons. The most important reason was to show our staff that we would enforce our vision and values in the face of this catastrophe. Firing Lorna showed the compliant employees that their adherence to the company values was respected and honored.

There are other times that an employee has been a good and loyal servant but, like a faithful horse that ages, cannot win the race anymore. Breaking ties with these employees is heart-wrenching because you love them and they love you. Our bookkeeper Nan fit this description. She was loyal, and when the company was small, she was excellent at her job. Nan aged alongside us and got to the point where she could not keep up, not even with help. She showed us love but got so cranky and ill-tempered that others couldn't work with her.

Nan wanted to retire but couldn't afford it. We figured out a way to give her an excellent severance retirement package and supplement her Medicare while she found a way to move to Mexico to live on what we offered. We cried, she cried, and eventually, she thrived, and the company thrived with a new bookkeeper. Asking her to retire was hard, but it was the right thing to do for everyone.

The Marines don't leave a man behind; they pick him up and take him to get help. First, they get him out of the line of fire, and then get him to safety. We needed to get Nan off the battlefield and off to Mexico.

**Lesson Learned:** A pit crew is like a choir—if one can't sing, then he's got to go.

BUCKLE UP FOR BUSINESS SUCCESS

Dad taught me not to get comfortable in the saddle. At an early age he had me take the reins and direct a team of horses.

# CHAPTER 18

# Desperation

*"Never let them know you're desperate."*

Destitution is the mother of recycling. When you can't buy anything, then you have to find what you need for free, and it is incredible what great finds you can dig up. Heck, being broke could even be fun, although I would never refer to 2008 as a fun year. We held onto an ink pen until that sucker went dry. We also learned that if you take out the plastic inside of the pen where the ink is, that you can bend it a little bit to squeeze the ink down to the tip and get a few more days out of it. Who needs highlighters when you can borrow the kids' crayons to underline information? If you peel a broken crayon and turn it lengthwise, it works exactly like a highlighter.

## BUCKLE UP FOR BUSINESS SUCCESS

Sticky notes can be made from scrap paper and taped on so one could give every minuscule unused piece of paper a function. There is no need for a legal tablet when you can reuse the backs of printer paper stapled together at the top. By stapling the paper on the side, recycled paper can turn into a notebook. The best idea is making your day-planning calendar with a ruler and number the days yourself. That alone saves 35 dollars or more.

One-ply toilet paper sucks, but that is what we used. Our office building was an old apartment building that creaked when we went from office to office. Our bathroom was right off the main office. The women in the office turned on the faucet so that the water running would drown the sound of tinkle in the toilet. Men didn't care about the sound; therefore, the noise was much like an elephant peeing on a rock.

The only thing missing from the office was rats. There were enough spiders to host a horror movie. To top it all off was the office worker that brought in bed bugs. It freaked the rest of us out so bad that we pooled our money to have the office fumigated.

FHB (family hold back) was the norm every payday. We all barely had enough for food, let alone pay our mortgages on time. We still had one child left at home that we managed to clothe thanks to hand-me-downs that came our way. Our dog even participated in the cutback by foregoing treats at night thanks to her owner's frugality.

The tightening didn't affect the purchase of vodka,

however. Rich somehow found hidden change for the cheapest bottle to find its way into the closet. The largest bottle possible drained dry within a few days. Drinking didn't affect his sales ability; alcohol consumption improved his spiel. He could sell ice to Eskimos by promising them that they could have a bonfire in their igloo without the ice melting. By the start of 2009, clients were coming our way again with promises that had us killing ourselves to keep.

The downturn in 2008 created an opportunity for our company. Dealerships found that we could do the job cheaper and better than what they could do themselves. If they chose to do the job in-house, they were replacing high-salaried administrators with undertrained clerical staff, thus creating a need for training—training that only I could provide. Rich was taking advantage of the open door and selling his ass off.

> **One thing is for sure: a child on drugs and a husband on booze is a recipe for catastrophe.**

We couldn't hire any more people because we did not have the revenue to support the extra salaries. I began traveling 48 weeks a year in 2009, training administrators across the U.S. I would get on a plane Sunday night, be working at the dealership eight to ten hours a day, go back to the hotel room at night and process overflow claims for our office. The trip ended with a hop, a late-night flight home on Friday nights. Saturday, I did mothering time for our budding daughter by fitting in a week's worth of girl bonding. Sunday was a family day until the household was ready for bed; that was my cue to get to the airport to repeat the routine all over again. I was worn out, but it began paying the bills. By the middle of 2010, the company was starting to turn around financially, but the home front was on a downward spiral.

Our daughter turned 15 years old, and high school proved to be a disaster from day one. Our sweet, compliant child was turning to drugs. It didn't help that I was still on the road, leaving her with a closet alcoholic parent. Rich didn't drink until everyone was in bed asleep, but the effects lingered into the morning more and more each day that went by. One thing is for sure—a child on drugs and a husband on booze is a recipe for catastrophe.

The crazy schedule I was on got more complicated with calls from home. Our crazy teen would call to complain about Rich being unreasonable. She was too angry to call him her father as she screamed into the phone, "Rich took my door off the hinge again because I slammed the door, but I didn't slam it. He thinks I have drugs in my room. He won't let me go over to my friend's house to study. I am going to study. Isn't that what you want me to do?"

Rich would take the phone away from her and start explaining, "She slammed the door so hard that the pictures fell off the wall. Moreover, yes, she is higher than a kite and won't stop screaming at me. Her friend is the one that got picked up by the cops for drugs."

I now added counselor to my list of duties, trying to pick my way through conversations and arguments, to get to the truth. I knew Rich was drinking. I knew my daughter was using drugs. That sweet child also knew which buttons she could push to fire him off. I knew we needed the money from what I was doing. For one second the thought went through my head, *What about me? Where are my needs here?* I quickly threw that out because I needed to be the grounding rod, not just for my family unit but for the company. Rich was selling ice to the Eskimos faster than people at the office could keep up. Everyone needed a piece of me, and I was not going to let anyone down.

There was new energy at the office. I was bringing back information from my trainings that further informed our own administrators. By training dealerships, I was advancing techniques for the training process in our own office. This fresh approach encouraged growth despite Rich's erratic behavior, which everyone chose to overlook.

The company was once again profitable by 2011. I was able to get off the road a few more weeks than in the past.

Rich wobbled into work each day. Our staff didn't know if he would remember what went on the previous day or not, so they started following up on every detail to make sure clients had their needs met. Our employees knew that one of two things would happen—Rich would either get mad because they reminded him, or he would do what they asked because he had no clue he forgot. Damn, he could sell no matter how messed up he was.

The hammer fell and hit us all one morning. At 7 a.m., Rich took his last drink and went back to bed for 30 minutes. After his nap, he stumbled into his clothes, unable to completely stand up. Preemptively, I had hidden the keys, knowing he would try to drive to work. "Give me the damn keys, Lisa," he said with his tone full of hatred. "Now, damn it."

> **Desperation will do one of two things: either cause potential buyers to shy away from your product, or send out a signal that they can get the product or service for less due to your need for the sale.**

This was when I called David. As David came to help out, Rich began yelling in the living room, "You two don't know what the hell you're talking about."

Our daughter chose this time to peek out of her room to add her two cents. "See, I told you he was crazy."

"You get back into your room right now and get ready for school." I peered sternly at her. "Crazy or not, you are getting your butt to school, and we will handle your dad."

David was finally able to talk Rich down and coach him back into bed. This same day, Rich left for rehab, David threw himself in the flames of sales, and I started mopping up the mess both at home and in the office.

David proved himself a natural at selling—when clients came to us for information. He was likable and honest; traits that people can feel in conversation. Neither David nor I were good at chasing a sale or finding new leads. Without people searching the company out, the new business coming in began to slow. We needed to network and to ask clients for contacts, but without our plea sounding desperate. Desperation will do one of two things: either cause potential buyers to shy away from your product, or send out a signal that they can get the product or service for less due to your need for the sale.

> **"Now, ask me when I would like to come on board."**

I searched out a friend in the business world that I could trust. Joe was a client, but also a friend who was honest and trustworthy. I sat down in his office and poured out my problems. Without crying, I put down each fact on his desk:

> *Rich was our salesperson and he was in rehab.*
> *I suck at sales.*

## BUCKLE UP FOR BUSINESS SUCCESS

*I have a kid at home out of control.*
*The company has 50 people depending on me to make sure they have work and a paycheck.*
*I am one person trying to do it all.*
*David is doing his best at sales and keeping our systems up and running.*

Then I described my sales technique to him. "You'll love our service. It is a bit pricey though; let me see if we can work out an affordable option."

Joe put his hand on top of mine and looked me in the eye. "Lisa, that is just one step up from saying, 'you don't want our service, do you?' You are worth more than this. Don't settle for less than what you are worth."

I looked down as Joe continued, "Never let them know you are desperate. Hold your head up and tell me what you are good at. Show me why I need your company. Now, ask me when I would like to come on board."

I looked at him, and with the wheels turning in my head, I answered, "That wasn't the sales pitch that I hear Rich giving. He brings in business, and I can't do what he does."

Joe smiled "You're not Rich, but you know that you are great at what you do. That is the best tool in your tool belt. All you have to do is tell clients the truth. Dealerships need you more than you need them. Don't sell yourself for less when you know you are worth more."

These words changed my view of sales. Desperation took a vacation and never returned to the business.

---

**Lesson Learned:** Racecar drivers keep the car on the road at all costs.

## CHAPTER 19

# Gut and Instinct— You Can't Explain It

*"God has a way of showing you where you need to grow. He was telling me to grow a zipper for my lips. Loose lips sink ships, and that ship sunk."*

Your stomach is a vital organ and can tell you much about your life. I have never tested for wheat intolerance or disease, but I can tell you that when I eat wheat, I bloat up like an old cow. I feel terrible, my pants won't fit, and because my pants are tight, I am cranky. I can eat bread but I know what is going to happen if I do, so I always ask myself, *Is it worth it?*

I learned how wheat makes me feel from experience, which enables me to recognize the mistake when I eat it again. Here is a true statement: Good judgment comes from experience. Experience comes from bad judgment. Your gut is what enables you to determine if a business deal is a right call or bad call. Your gut learns according to what you bring to the table, which in my case is not wheat.

Here is another story about Jake, because his gut is making the call based on our history together.

> **Your gut enables you to determine if a business deal is a right call or bad call.**

We had two administrators that worked on Jake's account at one time. They learned that we paid them roughly 45 percent of what Jake paid us. This is a good ratio in the service industry to cover computer costs, overhead, taxes, liabilities, and support staff. These two girls didn't calculate support financing into their equation. The number they saw made them think we were cheating them out of the other 55 percent. They calculated that they could go into business for themselves and keep 55 percent and be rich! They intended to start with Jake's accounts.

The two girls made an appointment to see Jake. Their first mistake was to show up in blue jeans and T-shirts that clashed with Jack's thousand-dollar suits; this visual started his gut churning.

The second mistake was their presentation. "We have been doing your account for the company and are doing an excellent job. We want to be able to do your account outside of the corporation, and we can charge you less than you are being billed, saving you money."

Because of Jake's ethics, this hit his gut like a bad meal of sushi rebelling in his stomach. He delivered his response with grace and a smile, "The reason I have Lisa's company do our work is when I have a problem with my account, I go directly to her for resolution. This means that I don't have to deal with people like you." He stood up to indicate the meeting was over. "Thank you for coming."

> **If someone would cheat on his or her current employer, guess what— he or she will do it to you, too.**

As soon as the room emptied, Jake called me. "Lisa, please replace the administrators working on my account. I need a person who will choose to make the correct decision with ethical boundaries."

Not all our clients would make this call because they don't have the same moral compass. When dealing with clients that don't have the instinct to do the right thing, you need your gut to come into play. If you are getting into bed with a client that would take the deal these girls were offering, your tummy should be churning with gas that is speaking these words: "Don't pull up the covers, this dude will fart and pull them over your head."

Jake was listening to his moral compass and refused to compromise the values his parents raised him with. The small voice inside warned him to watch for the danger ahead. This man's experience in life assured him that if someone would cheat on his or her current employer, guess what—he or she will do it to you, too.

Your gut will tell you not to give in to your desires. I equate this to going out to dinner when I am starving, and they bring crusty, fresh-baked bread with olive oil dipping sauce out before they take your order. My hunger is telling me to eat the food. My head is repeating, don't do it, you'll be sorry. I can't say that my head always wins, but when my hunger wins, my stomach loses.

An example of keeping your cool transpired as I was at a dealership. The computer company representative was describing to the dealer how the new submission process was going to work. He detailed the most significant improvements, adding, "The system is so slick that even a monkey can put in claims now. You don't need trained personnel."

First of all, the guy was an idiot to say that with me, the monkey, standing there. My temper wanted to shove his computer *where the sun don't shine*, but my gut told me to resist taking the bread and eating it. Instead of looking at his butt to shove the computer in, I looked him in the eye and said, "This is going to be a great tool for us administrators. We are going to have more time to make sure the data the monkey is putting in is correct and accurate. We can make our dealership more money because we can focus on bigger issues. I can't wait to try it."

On a side note, there are still no monkeys doing my job.

Now, I can give you an example where I went with the feral instinct that cost me a significant client for life. This behavior was early in my career, and my gut wasn't trained to know that the pain I was feeling was wheat. Mistakes aren't just forgotten—there is the duration of learning, and soaking them in. This one continues to absorb for 30-plus years.

> **He was telling me to grow a zipper for my lips. Loose lips sink ships, and that ship sunk.**

I had a large dealership group and worked well with all the staff in service. One day I arrived and found the department gutted of previous personnel, with only a few left standing. There was a new sheriff in town, and he brought his posse with him. He was an arrogant son-of-a-gun who spoke down to me, so I would know my place. I let my feelings get in the way and announced my distaste for the new sheriff to the remaining staff. That opinion made its way back to the new service manager, and I found myself fired. This small piece of gossip remained tucked into his memory for a lifetime. He continued at the dealership for the next 30 years, leaving me without a client for the 30 years. Had I listened to my gut, I would have known not to take the bait, but to let some time pass before spouting off. God has a way of showing you where you need to grow. He was telling me to grow a zipper for my lips. Loose lips sink ships, and that ship sunk. Sometimes you have to let things breath before you tackle them.

I have learned in business that when making a knee-jerk reaction, the result will almost always come back to bite you. Take the time you need to evaluate the proper response, and you will never have to relive the mistake your mouth makes.

Listen to your tummy when your head is telling you the wrong answers. I have the time to think for a minute before going full steam ahead. If it doesn't feel right, then it probably isn't right, at least in its present form.

**Lesson Learned:** Drivers believe in their instruments. When the check engine light comes on, pull over and have the engine inspected.

# CHAPTER 20

# Midnight Worship

*"Go over it, or under it, around it, or through it, but whatever you do, just do it."*

Rich spent his 60th birthday in rehab, and I didn't feel sorry for him one bit. His calls home were ugly because he blamed me for him being in rehab. It made me feel better to flip him off while he was on the phone ranting and raving—a gesture that he couldn't see. Our home was more relaxed, as I didn't have to worry about the stove being left on in the middle of the night. We were not afraid of some other exposure to safety due to Rich's forgetfulness due to the drinking. Our daughter was doing better without Rich yanking her up and down emotionally.

The evenings were the times when I allowed myself to

notice that the bottom had indeed fallen out of my life. I called it my midnight worship hour. I could cry out to God in my hopelessness, brokenness, and fear in this hour. My prayers were different because I opened my soul. Lamenting is an expression of the grief we hold inside. I lamented a lot! Finally, sleep could come, and daylight would allow me to conquer a new day with a new spirit. Putting some cucumber on the bags under my eyes, hid the torment of the night from the employees. Everyone has home problems, but the show must go on.

Both David and I learned valuable insights during this time.

> *We could do anything we set our minds to doing. Nothing was impossible.*
>
> *Relationships are built on honesty. We were honest about the service we would supply, and the timeframe involved.*
>
> *Clients will hang in there if you communicate before a hiccough happens. When we knew we would not be able to complete a job within the time limit of the promises that were made, we called the client right away.*

Failure wasn't an option. David let our clients know that we were experiencing a temporary management interruption due to medical circumstances. The work might be slower than usual, but it would get accomplished without impacting the quality they had come to expect. David's delivery and honesty were an invitation to our clients to come in closer as partners.

Without exception, every client gave us enough latitude to complete the work, running a few days behind what they customarily expected. Not only that, they referred other dealerships to us because of our integrity.

> **The bottom had indeed fallen out of my life. Everyone has home problems, but the show must go on.**

The last week of Rich's rehab arrived, and that meant we had to attend family week as part of his treatment. Not only were we behind at work, now David and I had to spend a week away from the office. Leaving the company shorthanded put another clog in the works. Three core people were not present to work the day-to-day issues for the company, posed a real liability. Somehow, we had to manage a juggling act to be productive on the road.

We dreaded the visit for several reasons—the biggest was working through family issues with the anger we still held toward Rich. Also, the conversations on the phone were less than favorable.

David, our daughter, and I arrived at the center for visitation without fanfare. We didn't feel like hugging the jerk, and jerk-face didn't feel like hugging us. Wow, this was going to be a great week. His first words were, "Have you all screwed up the company yet?"

The sentence hit my "screw you" button and started the week with a bang. Both David and I looked at each other, silently agreeing that Rich was the one that put the company in jeopardy. We were working our asses off to pull it out of the tar pit.

Anger, sadness, and loneliness arose in the kind of cry that makes you cover your face with a towel so no one can see you. The heaving of my emotions came out in a brief ten minutes that left me tired but invigorated with determination to succeed. We would attend the required workshops, and then get back to the business of working for the company after hours.

> **Having a company is an endurance race. This lap could have turned into a demolition derby, instead of completing the circuit.**

We all three—David, our daughter, and I—attended the family therapy classes, learning about Rich's behavior. The dry-drunk period where he still acted like he did when he was drunk. We were to expect a healing period of irrational thinking and the overall craziness of living with an alcoholic. Yep, we knew what to expect, but none of us liked what we saw. Rich's words and actions sounded like the same old thing, just a different day. Great!

Rich came home and resumed his sales work, not always remembering what he promised each client, but the revenue returned while David and I followed up carefully to make sure that the work and promises were fulfilled as stated. The roles were now reversed, with David, the son, picking up after the parent. Picture in your mind how a parent follows a toddler around the house picking up toys, and you can envision our task.

The business was booming again, however. Rich was healing. He had enough stubbornness in him that he would never take another drink. But the lifelong addiction would continue to haunt him throughout his recovery.

David's growth in knowledge and capability was a huge byproduct of his father's problems. The incident gave him confidence in his own ability. The company was making money only by the grace of God and the grit that we were putting in.

Every business owner has personal problems. Each has family issues to deal with. Life isn't perfect. We learned that having a company is an endurance race. This lap could have quickly turned into a demolition derby, instead of completing the circuit.

. . . . . . . . . . . . . . . . . . . . . . . . . . . . . . . . . . . . . . . . . . . . . . .

**Lesson Learned:** In driving school, you learn to keep your hands at 9 and 3 o'clock positions. Don't let go. Even if your arms get all twisted.

# CHAPTER 21

# Don't Be a Dumbass

*"A dumbass is someone who attempts to be a smartass but is too dumb to actually succeed."*

You will never make it in business being a dumbass, a smartass, a lazyass, or a jackass.

We all do dumb things but being a dumbass is much more than just doing stupid stuff now and again—we all do that.

In the Urban Dictionary, a dumbass is someone who looks up the word "dumbass" in the dictionary. That means that right now, I am acting like a dumbass.

A dumbass in this case is not thinking inside or outside of the box. It is answering before you think about the consequences.

My teen daughter used to try to push me into a corner with my answers, wanting me to be a dumbass so she could get her way. "Mom, we are just going to a place to dance. They don't have drugs or alcohol; it's not a place like that. It is just two hours: that is it. Two hours! Why can't I go for two hours?"

> **"If you have to push me into an answer right now, the answer is no."**

I learned that if I said, "No, there is no way you are going there," she might sneak out or spend the night with a friend (parents, you know what that means.)

If I replied, "Yes, but I need to check it out," the place might not check out, and I would need to go back to "no, you can't go." That put me in a position of going back on my word.

The best reply was not to be a dumbass and let her put me in that position, and instead responding, "If you have to push me into an answer right now, the answer is no. However, if you give me a bit to check it out, the answer might be different. It's your choice; would you like an answer now or give me investigation time?"

I would watch her as she mulled those two choices over in her mind. Her eyes would squint, and she twitched her mouth to the side. Then impatiently she blurted, "OK, then!

I'll wait, but can you please hurry and decide?" The same goes in business; the answer doesn't need to be immediate. You can inform clients, employees, or whoever, that you are going to need sometime before answering.

> **Embarrassment is what happens when you put a smartass with a dumbass.**

A smartass will respond to situations with sarcasm. I had one case when we were dealing with a dealership in Alaska, and every repair they performed on a vehicle was overkill. For example, if one shock needed replacing, then we would get a claim with all four shocks replaced with no reason why they all needed to be installed. Customers came to the shop with a no start, and the car would get an overhaul with a new starter, battery and, in some cases, a whole engine. When we would inquire about the necessity, the service manager almost always had the same reply: "This is Alaska, and everything is different here. If one shock is bad, we assume they will all go out. If that should happen, the customer will be in the middle of open tundra."

One of our administrators got a similar reply in email form and forwarded me the response with her name at the bottom, and this smartass salutation: "Retards!"

I was a dumbass and thought it said, "Regards!"

I forwarded the email with "Retards" in the salutation to the service manager, stating we needed a better explanation for all four shocks.

She sent the explanation back, stating replacement was necessary because all four shocks were leaking, and signed it, "From the Retards in Alaska."

Embarrassment is what happens when you put a smartass with a dumbass.

A lazyass or a jackass will not make it very far in business. Both of these types will be average or below unless they are lucky and just fake their way along.

> **Lazy people don't work hard enough to make a commission, and so they soon wash out.**

We had one administrator that lumbered around shuffling his feet everywhere he went. He did just enough to get by so we could not fire his lazyass. These types of employees needed a full-time manager that could set clear goals and make sure they were met in a timely fashion. Once we did this, the employee was not able to complete the task, and the inferior work was documented so we could let him go.

I really do hate trying to motivate lazy people. For crying out loud, I put more work into making sure that they work than they do! Since our company model is commission-based, the lazyasses don't last long. Our pay is based on "you eat what you kill." In other words, you make the money; you get to keep the money. Lazy people don't work hard enough to make a commission, and so they soon wash out.

If your company works on hourly or salary, the lazy employee has to work under these guidelines:

> *Specific goals must be written out with steps for achievement.*
>
> *The goals must be measurable and have a value.*
>
> *You must make the goal achievable but don't cut any slack—your expectations should be the same as for a non-lazyass.*
>
> *Finally, the manager must set a time limit and make sure that timeline is enforced.*

We also have had a jackass that we kept on staff. He thought that holding back from stating negatives made him a nice person. His voice was louder than others on the floor. He believed the world is full of jerks, and he was just projecting his voice above the other jerks. Anger was his most useful tool until you properly made him shut up.

He led a small team that kept shrinking because he didn't trust his teammates. However, he was good at keeping his mouth in check with clients, and they believed he was terrific.

What this shows me is that jackasses can control themselves when they have that desire. A jackass is a workhorse; they can carry a lot of weight. But they are stubborn and loud, and you have to know how to work with them.

Managing a jackass is not impossible. You need to be to the point, state what you insist on with as few words as possible and hold the arrogant ass accountable.

Here is a litmus test for a business to see which ass you employ:

> The problem:
>
> To process the paperwork for a client, you must provide the manufacturer with specific items. You are the expert in knowing which details must have documentation and within what time limits. Not only that, YOU get paid a percentage of what the client receives refunded for the claim.
>
> Example: Claim 12345
>
> *Needs a part charged out for a clamp that was replaced.*
>
> *The technician must have a reference number for the document he used, containing instructions for the repair.*
>
> *Neither of these items is present.*

Dumbass will send an email for the part to be charged out and forget to include information about the reference number. Leaving out essential details will mean that the dummy will have to email again for another reason once the dealer adds the part.

Smartass sends an email stating, "If you used the part, why didn't you put it in the ticket? You read the instructions, so why didn't you put it in the comments?"

Lazyass waits days for a return email and doesn't follow up because it's too much trouble to see if the email went to the right person.

> **The Notanass makes $1,000 for his cut for the effort while Dumbass, Smartass, Lazy Ass, and Jackass go hungry.**

Jackass figures that if the client doesn't put down the right information, it serves him right not to get the money. It's not his fault that they are too stupid to put the correct information in the claim.

That is why it is better to be a Notanass. Help others succeed so you can achieve.

A Notanass would handle the same scenario by doing the following:

> *Send an email with a subject line (Information needed on 12345).*
>
> *Include bullet points for each item required and the timeframe.*
>
> *Sign with gratitude in advance for the assistance.*
>
> *Include his or her name and contact information*

After 24 hours, the notanass would do a follow-up phone call to make sure the email was received and offer support in solving the problem.

The notanass makes $1,000 for his cut for the effort while Dumbass, Smartass, Lazy Ass, and Jackass go hungry.

The above story is the grown-up version of "The Little Red Hen."

. . . . . . . . . . . . . . . . . . . . . . . . . . . . . . . . . . . . . . . . . . . . . .

**Lesson Learned:** Racecar drivers don't email the pit crew during a lap because the car needs tires. There is no room for laziness in the pit.

# CHAPTER 22

# Healing from Reeling

*"You cannot hold on to feelings of sadness
and disappointment because doing so means
you are blocking what life has to offer."*

Rich came home with a renewed passion for the company. He jumped back into sales, only this time he remembered the calls. When he spoke with a potential client, he was in an altered state, talking in what the Bible would refer to as "tongues." Words came out as smooth as the sound from a snake charmer's flute, enticing dealers to sign up for our services. Rich's mind was slowly healing from the years of alcohol, but each day, his thoughts showed more clarity. Work was invigorating and giving him purpose.

Business came in fast and furious. Our administrators

were processing paperwork in a sea of assholes and elbows, collecting money for the dealerships. All hands were on deck. If you could breathe, then you could process paperwork. Our managers weren't managing; they were processing claims. David was processing claims, and I was processing claims; we even had the dog lying on papers as a paperweight. The thought briefly crossed my mind to try to put a pen in our furry friend's paw.

We were too busy working accounts to teach new people properly. Our motto was if the person was warm and breathing, not from our church, and not a vampire, then we were going to hire him. We knew this was not an intelligent hiring process, but we figured even if five out of ten people worked out, then we were still ahead of the ball. The company was drinking from a fire hydrant. At one point, I remember holding one of the grandbabies with one arm, feeding him from a bottle held under my chin while the other hand worked the computer. I had the phone cradled between the bottle, my jaw, and my shoulder while I discussed a ticket with a client. The puppy thought playtime had arrived and was pulling on my pant legs, growling. Even with all the commotion, this was a calm day. I couldn't help but break out into song, *Cause I'm a Woman. W O M A N.*

Mistakes became frequent with our new, warm, and breathing bodies—until the fateful day that I calmly took my arm and swung it across my desk to clear all the piles of papers in one smooth swoop. The company had reached a breaking point. The *I Love Lucy* skit where Lucy and

Ethel are working in the candy factory is comparable to the position we found ourselves in. In the show, the candy came faster and faster on the conveyor belt, and Lucy and Ethel could not keep up. They frantically started shoving candy in their mouths and in their clothes and anywhere they could to get rid of the candy. That is precisely how our employees felt.

> **We had a "which comes first, the chicken or the egg?" problem.**

We had to cut off sales to regroup and establish management. We needed processes to follow and the right people in place to carry them out. Even with the right people in place, there needed to be a guideline for training them. We couldn't continue throwing good people into the lion's den to be eaten alive. We found humor in our inside joke that we could take three new people, name them Shadrach, Meshach, and Abednego, then throw them into the fire of claims processing and see if they could walk out.

Rich, our marvelous snake charmer, needed to put the snake back in the basket for a while. Turn the sales faucet off so we could get enough people to do the work. That is when we discovered our real problem—do we stock up on people, hoping that work will come in, or get the job first, and then hire the people? We had a *which comes first, the chicken or the egg* problem. Finding the right balance of people and business is part of the growing pains that you will experience as success overtakes your company.

A lack of knowing how to manage and train properly kept us in a continuous loop.

> *Turn the sales faucet on—to fill up the administrators we hired.*
> *Turn the sales faucet off—so we can hire another person to train.*
> *Turn it on.*
> *Turn it off.*

> **Finding the right balance of people and business is part of the growing pains that you will experience as success overtakes your company.**

This frustrated Rich, our only sales guy. As he explained, "When you tell me to turn off sales and put the client off for an unspecified time, they will lose interest and go elsewhere. Then when you tell me to turn it on again, it isn't like sales magically appear. It takes time for the flow to start. I have to start a courting process all over again, and that can take months. By the time I have sales running again, you tell me to turn new business off, and the leads go cold. It's like dating—by the time you get to second base with the girl, she says you're out before you can get to home plate."

We were managing by crisis, but how could we ever get ahead of the curve without cash to fund new bodies before we needed them? Moreover, what in the heck would we have employees do if the client wasn't in the door yet and they had no work to do? We couldn't afford to have people just sitting around with no job, for heaven's sake!

The thought of taking on another partner for cash was out of the question. Both Rich and I got the shivers thinking about how that ended—escorted out the door of the previous company.

If we lost a person while in the water faucet dance, we were screwed and had to start all over again. We were not getting anywhere fast.

Rich had always been the risk-taker in our family and business. So far, those risks had sent us to the poor farm several times, but he had never been this sober before. I also thought back to the risks he took that paid off. Telling the truth to Jake about his $16,000 mistake was a risk. Starting over was a huge risk. Getting money from the banker was a risk. I figured that I was in a love/hate relationship with Rich's gambles.

I am the creative developer on the team. Rich and I are both high "D" for dominant in the DISC personality assessment; this means each of us will fight to the death for our way. My D is tempered with a high C for creative. Rich's personality is just a D—off-the-chart high D. Literally, the D is off the IDAK chart. Many high-spirited conversations about the company flowed through our home in the evenings. All businesses need a D person, but they also need all the other combinations of employees to temper the functionality of the company and keep all machinery running.

I had to design a training program for our company administrators—a systematic approach to warranty administration that was similar to the Powertraining© program we created for a dealership. We needed a classroom-type training which scheduled completion in two weeks, with one week spent in a class environment and the second week hands-on. Having a system of training and apprenticeship meant that we would only be out money for salary for one week, and the second week could have some payout. There was a risk, but not a huge risk. The outcome, if all went well, would be a win.

Rich's idea was to bring in a dozen new administrators at a time to get things rolling. I fought back, reasoning that this was a new program not yet tried. Also, the price tag would be far too high, for the company to absorb. Ten people times a salary for the first few weeks was a substantial economic strain to our cash flow. The price for labor, coupled with the impossibility of properly working with that many administrators at once to do an adequate job was not achievable. We needed a smaller student-to-teacher ratio for new administrators to reach a proficient skill level. One more thing—I didn't want to go broke yet again. I liked eating regularly. More head-butting occurred before we compromised on a suitable size class of two to four unskilled students for the trial run.

I started the curriculum with a class syllabus. Next, I developed course material for each day and a workbook for the students. I included a check sheet for the mentor to complete for the following week, listing each skill the apprentice needed before graduating to process claims on his or her own. I assembled the complete curriculum in a notebook that had an expandable index and room for screenshots and notes for each new employee. I was the teacher. I had taught hundreds of administrators to do this job working one-on-one with them in their dealerships. How hard could a classroom be?

Hard!

I can read to children, talk to them, and perform on cue. There is no judgment by little people. You can get away with anything, and they still hug you when class is over.

Public speaking with adults is quite another situation. Adults stare at you when you are talking and, all of a sudden, I feel I am boring them. I don't want to talk down to them, so I speed up my speaking, not realizing I am leaving them behind. Here are some things I learned to help me be a better teacher:

> *Be passionate. I am passionate about my business, so why wasn't I letting it show? It felt dumb to be excited about pushing paper, but doggone it, I am. So I went for it.*

> *Invite others to speak, but control the floor and the time. Asking questions helps share ideas, and I learned a thing or two in a few classes.*
>
> *Slow down. You don't need to finish a five-day course in three days. Empty seconds are okay. Give people time to think.*
>
> *Use humor if you can. No one wants to see an annoying slide show for eight hours. Use a funny film clip or picture to wake up the class.*
>
> *Games are suitable for small groups. I purchased a deck of cards to play poker. Every time someone answered a question, they got a playing card—the best hand in five-card stud received a coffee gift card.*

Our first class was a success. Two out of our four new administrators were ready to start processing paperwork by the second week, right on schedule. They were assigned a mentor to work with for the next five days before we assigned them their accounts. The other two employees in the class needed more mentoring before being assigned client. The result of the coaching was great information and an opportunity to develop team leaders to watch over and tutor the administrators that needed the extra time learning the new skill.

> **In your own business, you have to find that sweet spot for employees and clients.**

We had the next class scheduled on the heels of the first class. The process took on a life of its own with classes beginning every month. The class size increased to five to six employees since our school environment was a success.

Rich was smiling and dialing again. His phone was his flute, enticing the snakes out of the basket. Work was coming in steadily. We scheduled our classes once a month. We didn't go broke, because we planned adequately and had a stable process to accomplish the goal. In your own business, you have to find that sweet spot for employees and clients. The plan may look different, depending on your product.

Laura Ingalls Wilder wrote something that I read once, and I have never been able to find it since. It went something like this: *You start paying for things long before you buy them.* The words are not an exact quote, but the meaning is the same.

It cost our company a year's worth of business because we didn't spend the money on a training course sooner. The same is true in our everyday lives, too, and I have seen it many times. We had a crack in our wall where the closet was coming loose, so I decided to caulk it because I didn't want to spend the money to have someone fix it. Then one day, the whole closet fell off the wall. If I had hired someone to fix it when we spotted the crack, it would have required a few screws to be adjusted. Now, we had to have the whole wall rebuilt. I found out that being a good steward of the money is a great thing, but being a cheapass is almost as bad as being a dumbass or a lazyass.

**Lesson Learned:** A racecar needs new tires for the race, even if the old ones still have tread on them.

# CHAPTER 23

# Viewpoint is Everything

*"Your managers can be bitches or angels, depending on an employee's viewpoint."*

Compassion for others is a necessity in business. The Family and Medical Leave Act protects an employee's job with unpaid leave for employees with a severe medical condition. Having protection for your position is essential, but the employee will not have income during that period, and I can assure you that the majority of your staff has no stash of cash to get them through surgery or a medical condition while they are off work. Compassion drives us to help the ones who cannot help themselves, but small or medium-sized businesses do not have the resources to put compassion into action. Even when your financials have positive numbers, your cash flow can still be tight.

Our company determined that minor adjustments could allow us to put our sorrow into action. We offer a third-party voluntary insurance policy for short-term disability, maternity, and illness that can be subtracted from our employees' checks, with direct payments sent to the insurance company. The insurance allows employees to plan for emergencies and be able to take care of their own needs. Being self-dependent is the optimal choice and will give employees and their family security. Opting to provide financial investment for your staff costs your company zero but will be appreciated by many of your employees.

These policies will never cover all the expenses the same as a paycheck. I previously mentioned that our company has chosen to reserve and set aside two days of severe medical leave for our employees each year, which can be used in the event of a condition that leaves them unable to work for an extended period. It is not a "take it with you policy" or worth cash value outside of our company. We have made sure to describe it this way legally, emphasizing it is a catastrophic self-insurance agreement.

Since life is interesting and people are wacky, the viewpoint on disability can get skewed. Humans are the most bizarre animals on earth. One human has logic and sensibility, while the next person seems to be lacking the ability to see the world through a clear lens. The logical human will see a good manager as someone that watches over him. Inspecting his work and offering a guiding hand through storms, the manager approves vacations, assistance, and sick time.

> **The logical human will see a good manager as someone that watches over them. An employee with foggy glasses sees the same manager as a witch or warlock that continually hounds them, insisting that the job be completed.**

An employee with foggy glasses sees the same manager as a witch or warlock that continually hounds him, insisting that the job be completed. This worker has a self-view of life with sentences that most always start with "I." "I need the day off. I can't work today. I have soccer practice. I don't want to call the client; the client has to call me. I don't have time."

Veronica is one employee that was logical and needed to take advantage of the critical medical agreement due to suffering a minor stroke. Her years in the company meant that she had 20 days in the bank. I say minor stroke because she was still able to walk and talk, but her motor skills and mental recall were severely affected.

This terrific woman was one of our most valuable and

loyal employees. Her fellow workers and managers loved Veronica. A smiling redhead, she greeted fellow workers via phone or computer program, and they knew each day her joy would spill, overflowing to them. Her work was impeccable, and her clients' satisfaction was through the roof. Veronica worked extra hours when needed, and she saw her clients as her extended family. Many times, she would cry over their heartache or rejoice in their celebrations. Her teammates and clients were heartbroken when she suffered her stroke. To add to the seriousness of her financial situation, her husband had recently lost his job and they had adopted a child only a year before. Having the insurance policy helped, but the extra 20 days of pay relieved her mind of worry for at least 20 days, plus her three weeks of paid time.

Veronica had a slow healing process, but the 23 weeks allowed her time for recovery and physical therapy, facilitating her return to work part-time as she continued to get her short-term memory back. Today she is fully recovered and has earned a position as one of our top leaders, managing a successful team of administrators. Veronica views her supervisor with wings hovering above as she performs her work diligently.

> **Some individuals are not capable of time management.**

This model has been used many times as our employee's battle cancer or other debilitating illnesses. It doesn't cost the company much monetarily but it allows us to contribute to humanity.

Let's switch gears now to the employees that want you to have compassion for the craziest circumstances that they created by their own choices. These are the times when we scratch our heads and mutter aloud, "What the heck is wrong with people?"

Teri was one of those people who couldn't seem to complete her workload due to her life choices. Most of our administrators work from home and are located all over the U. S. Working from home improves productivity in most cases and eliminates commute times and expenses. However, some individuals are not capable of time management. Teri's work was never completed on time; consequently, we did a time study, looking at her computer log time. Her manager found that she was not working most of the day.

Teri had an attitude when confronted. "Well, I work when I can!"

Her manager was taken aback. "What do you mean, you work when you can? We have a signed contract with you confirming our hours are 8:00 to 5:00. You agreed to work those hours."

With a gruff, loud voice, Teri continued, "I have goats living in my house! My allergies are going crazy, I can't stop sneezing, and the noise is driving me crazy. I can't concentrate on working! Yesterday I had to take my boy to a

4H meeting right in the middle of the day. Every single day I have to take the kids to school. It takes me an hour and a half each way. So when am I supposed to work?" (Notice those I words?)

The manager's first instinct was to laugh because she hoped Teri was joking, but with Teri's attitude, she realized this was not a joke. Teri was actually mad at her manager because she made poor life choices.

> **"Your life choices are not my problem. My problem is that you are not working during the hours you were hired to work."**

Thankfully, my production manager made a quick recovery after the initial shock. "Your life choices are not my problem. My problem is that you are not working during the hours you were hired to work. You have 24 hours to make different choices, or you will need to find a job that fits your lifestyle. It isn't the company's obligation to adjust the job to your lifestyle. You have to adjust your lifestyle to fit the job to stay employed."

Teri now thinks that the manager is a bitch for not understanding her circumstances, while Veronica thinks the same manager is an angel. The comedian Ron White was right when he said, "You can't fix stupid." Our policy for compassion remains for those truly in need and without goats living in their house.

We learned a valuable lesson in that the programs need to state what circumstances the benefit covers in the employee handbook. Review your manual yearly. There are companies and councils that you can hire for a minimal charge to review the verbiage to keep the company compliant. Yes, you may have to put a contingency in for goats.

**Lesson Learned:** On a racetrack, corners are never fair.

# CHAPTER 24

# Embracing Technology

*"You better get on the bus, because the bus is leavin', with or without you."*

When I think back to the technology that was available when I started my career, it brings home just how old I am. I began my career with handwritten information on a paper ticket. The next step was transferring information that the technician provided. The pricing on the card was added, multiplied, divided, and totaled on a calculator that made printing noises as it printed the numbers on a feeder tape. The process was laborious and time-consuming.

> **Candy is a great tool, one that is every bit as useful as a hammer.**

We thought technology was fabulous when part numbers and pictures were on microfiche. For those who don't know what this is, microfiche held information on little cards that resembled negatives of old photographs. The cards were entered into a reader that magnified the information onto a bright screen so you could read it. This machine gave me nightmares that my family photographs were only available on microfiche cards, and I couldn't see them anymore. Funny that I still remember that dream, since nowadays our photos are only available on our phones. One could consider that a dream come true.

I spoke earlier about receiving $10,000 for a chocolate bar, but technology changes, our jobs evolve, and our tool belt now has more than a hammer and a screwdriver. Back in the day, candy was a staple for every bag of claims mailed to the automobile manufacturer. The visual of a hard-working claims administrator finding a much-needed chocolate break made me smile. Hershey was my new tool, and I wielded it with finesse.

By the way, candy is still a great tool, one that is every bit as useful as a hammer.

> **If the tool fits your morals and values, then use the dang thing. Put your thinking cap on.**

No matter what decade you live in or what the next generation brings, there are going to be new and improved tools coming along. However, no matter how many power tools are invented, the hammer is still one of the most useful items in the garage. That fact brings home the importance of never forgetting how to do a task in the old-fashioned way if a necessity arises.

I use this example in many stories about having the right tool to do the job. If you don't have the right tools, it is your responsibility to get the proper tool. Coming to work with the appropriate equipment is your problem; no one is going to give you the tools. Nothing is impossible. If the tool fits your morals and values, then use the dang thing. Put your thinking cap on. Chocolate bars are definitely within my values, so I used them to the fullest extent during the winter months. Mailing the candy during the summer would only reap a melted mess (a lesson in when you should use your tools!).

When I first started in the car business, my sweet success earned me the top producer spot at Hertz several years in a row. I was now the proud owner of a glossy 8 x 10 photo of OJ Simpson and me. At the time, OJ was the Hertz spokesperson and could be seen running through the airports to rent a Hertz vehicle to get to his next event. He was a big deal before he was on trial for murder. I put the picture away now, as I feel it is nothing to display proudly.

Technology took a big leap with computers. We typed data into computers with 10 x 10 floppy disks that stored, sent, and read data. We would use one floppy to input the data, take that one out and put another in to copy the information, and used a third to send the data. We thought floppy disks were the greatest thing since sliced bread! It saved a bundle on chocolate bars.

Our son David has always been our technical geek. It started while he was in the Marine Corps with nothing to do. Collapsing during a training exercise, he passed out with his heart rate over 240 beats per minute. Once in medical, the limited staff in the field could not regulate his rhythm or bring down his heart rate. Further testing at the hospital determined he had developed heart problems while serving on active duty. With one surgery at Bethesda Naval Hospital that minimized the condition, they slapped a heart monitor on him and relegated him to light duty. He was bored out of his mind and told me, "I am a professional bullshitter. I sit in a rolling chair and bullshit all day. They won't discharge me until I am stable. I am bored out of my mind."

I had a wild idea of sending him computer manuals to read to see if he had any interest in the new-fangled equipment once he got out of the service. David devoured the material and kept asking for more information. His infatuation started with a computer manual for dummies. Once out from under active duty for Uncle Sam, he attended computer school, and it has been his love ever since. David's mind is analytical. When you look closely into his eyes, you can see gears turning as they go through a methodical checklist of how things work.

For the new company in 2014, David created our CARS program—Claim Accountability Reporting System. We walked into the office one morning to find him slumped over three six-foot whiteboards with mathematical equations scribbled on every inch of space. He looked much like a crazy inventor with his messy auburn hair and crumpled clothes. David knew he had invented a game-changer. A smile with perfectly straight teeth peeked through the red-haired stubble of the night's growth on his face.

A massive problem in the industry was staying compliant with the manufacturers' policies and procedures. We attached red and yellow tags to the paperwork that we sent by mail or runner to our dealerships, indicating the non-compliance issue(s) to be corrected. The red cards had a message as to why the repair could not be submitted to the manufacturer. The yellow tags had warnings that the claim was paid; however, if the manufacturer came to look at the paperwork, they would most likely take the money back. This system was known as our claim accountability system. The red and yellow tags were a product that we developed during our Powertraining© at the dealerships in previous years. The system was genius because the stickers alerted management where their holes were and how to operate more efficiently within the guidelines.

David's design put the compliance system of the red and yellow tag concept into a computer program that would allow information to be transmitted to the dealerships by email. The program kept items open until answered and would compile a report weekly to show managers where the weakest link in their department resided. He developed a dashboard for the dealership to work from, eliminating the need to hunt for emails.

> **Like any other technological advance, some people met our tech alien creature with resistance.**

We hired a programmer to bring David's creation to life. The new system allowed our administrators to do more work, the work got more manageable, and the dealerships had a management tool to stay compliant with the manufacturer. This system was and still is cutting edge for the automobile warranty industry.

Our company had a system that no other claims management organization had. We were already a leader in the industry, but now we had a proprietary system that blew the doors off the competition.

Like any other technological advance, some people met our tech alien creature with resistance. Naysayers said, "It's too hard, it's just one more thing I have to do or look at." David's response was, "It's just like email. Instead of handwriting the answer on a paper tag, you type the answer into the computer, then the system will do the rest for you. The program sends the answer, tracks it, and keeps a record for access." After many battles, our dealers and administrators started to get on board.

We named David's incredible creature CARS, and using the program a mandatory condition of employment. We were all going toward the same goal, and we needed the entire group to go our direction. We told the obstinate employees that silently refused to use the new tool, "The Company is going in this direction whether you like it or not, so you better get on the bus, because the bus is leavin', with or without you."

It took a strict approach of zero tolerance to move the ball. Yes, we had to let outstanding people go because they felt the policy didn't apply to them with an attitude of "I am so good, they will never let me go." Well, we did because they were so good and ripe, they became rotten.

The problem with technology is that it is hard for people to let go and move on to the next best thing. A little coaching and Hershey's chocolate can be one of the most excellent tools you own.

Encourage creativity. Know when to enforce a new policy. Find simple tools to overcome adversity.

---

**Lesson Learned:** Drivers, keep your eyes up here, on that big thing above the dashboard—the windshield.

# LISA REINICKE

The picture that I keep put away of me and O J-
This award was a big deal and at the time, O J was
a big star. This was long before his poor wife was
murdered and the glove was found didn't fit.

# CHAPTER 25

# Peacock Suits

*"A peacock has beautiful plume when
showing off, but underneath the
colorful feathers is an ugly old bird."*

Hiring employees is a crapshoot, at best. With everything online now from the search to the resume to the first interview, it's hard to know what you are going to get in a person. Heck, sometimes that first interview is online now, via video.

What looks good on paper doesn't always reflect the person you are going to see when he or she arrives at your doorstep. You attempt to go through all the right steps outlined in the books that you read, the webinars you attended, or coaching and classes you visited. Maybe you have a human resource manager that is in charge, and you think that job is a piece of cake because HR's only real job is to bring in potential candidates.

> **"Birds fly, fish swim, and people do what they are wired to do!"**

You might use personality tests or other compatibility quizzes to see if potential employees will succeed in the position needed or in the company in general. I had one consultant explain the reason he wanted us to use his evaluation questions. With a cocky sideways grin, he said, "Birds fly, fish swim, and people do what they are wired to do. That is why you must test them before you hire them." Then in the next hour I spent with him he said, "Birds fly, fish swim, and people do what they are wired to do" at least 20 more times. The saying became a joke with all my managers. "You know why it didn't work? Birds fly, fish swim, and people do what they are wired to do!"

Don't get me wrong, this type of testing and the data it produces can be valuable when hiring and managing personnel. However, you can have a person that is wired to be an accountant, but if he has a crappy work ethic, he will still be a crappy accountant no matter how he is wired. Birds do fly, but I don't like the ones that build nests in my flower pots. Fish swim, but the ones that don't swim well eventually will float to the top on their sides.

Once you have completed your due diligence by evaluating the resume, initial contact, and possibly testing, you are ready for the first interview. The prospect arrives nicely dressed (or not) and makes an excellent first impression. Your thoughts are favorable for hiring the candidate.

> **Do call references, but remember they are not an entirely accurate picture of who the person is in all cases.**

The next step is to call the references. Joe Schmo, the manager at his last job, quickly answers, "Oh ya, fine guy." On the next call, Vicki Voo, the other employer, says, "Yes, this is a good person, and he did some temp work for us." Finally, you call the personal reference, Gushy Gerty, who raves, "He is the finest person. He loves small children and dogs, so that tells you what kind of guy he is."

The problem with references is that Gushy Gerty is his bestie (best friend). Joe wants to get him off their unemployment, and Vicki only worked with him a short time. Do call references, but remember they are not an entirely accurate picture of who the person is in all cases.

At this point, you do a second interview, and you are

now at least two weeks into needling that new person to fill your position. You know that if the potential employee has any scruples, he will give two weeks' notice. A month into this process, you might have the job filled—if you are lucky. That can set any business or department back, especially if you are a smaller company. All flags seem to be waving for you to hire the candidate, so you do.

That first day arrives, your new employee starts work, and it looks like things are going to be good. The week goes on; it still appears all is well. As the relationship eases, the new person eventually takes off his peacock suit, and you find out that it is just an ugly old bird.

Most of the best hires we ever had came from the first impression—from the gut. We then did all the precautions above to vet the prospect, but that first feeling in the pit of your stomach can tell you a lot.

One such applicant, Jackie, is an example of a gut instinct. We called her to schedule an urgent interview because the position had a deadline. "I can get there right now," she told us, "although I am not dressed for an interview. I was out running errands in my jeans. I can get there now or run home to change clothes first."

We are a pretty relaxed company, so I answered, "No, come on in, we are good now; jeans are acceptable, and we won't judge." Jackie was honest from the get-go. She was willing to do what we needed her to do. That small window gave me insight into her character.

> **If you are not crystal clear about what you, the employer, want in the role, how are you ever going to determine whether your candidates possess those skills?**

Another thing that will assist the company in developing a long-term employee is to ensure that you have a clear job description for the potential new hire. Now is the time to have a conversation about what the position is supposed to accomplish. If you are not crystal clear about what you, the employer, want in the role, how are you ever going to determine whether your candidates possess those skills?

There is no acceptable excuse for why an interviewer has not studied each resume and identified areas in the biography to explore in the interview. There is no reason why the questions you ask each candidate aren't prepared in advance and related to the skills in the job description. Anyone who asks, "So tell me about yourself…" is unprepared for this or any interview.

Do a short map of your new hire process with a starting point and ending point. List the stopping points along the way, such as getting gas, red lights, and landmarks. If you design a good map, then you will know your way every single time without getting lost. Here is an example that we use:

*The gas to go: The potential employee must have five years of experience before we consider hiring as a telecommuter administrator*

*Red light: talks poorly about the previous employer*

*Landmark: has worked with a client we know*

Since those old days of hiring anything that had two legs and a head, we have learned a few things.

> **If the candidate answers negatively and complains about the prior manager or company, then he or she will do the same to you when the job doesn't work out.**

Not having enough experience in the automobile industry will lead a new work-from-home employee to the death march to unemployment. Sending people home to work without the energy of helpful minds within touching distance isn't fair to our company or the employee. We set them up for failure. In times before, we have broken this golden rule only to find out why we made the rule in the first place. Now, we are firm that this will be the gas to say, "Let's pursue this potential hire further."

In the interview process, we ask the question, "Why

that were spent correcting issues. Now add in the money that could have been made as revenue to that figure. It puts a whole new perspective on what you can afford.

There are times we are scared of that department. What if we fire them? What if they quit? We won't be able to work, and then we will all starve to death because we won't have their passwords…and so on.

We have had failures in IT and technical development. One team came in and built a maze and a fortress in an unused portion of the offices. This is not a metaphor maze and fortress I am talking about. There were three little amigos in our IT areawho decided to keep all the riff-raff out by building a structure with leftover cubical walls so they could not be bothered to fix the staff's IT issues. The three were tight as thieves and refused to repair a computer without a proper ticket delivered by email.

With four layers of walls, it was as if they dared me to do anything about the entanglement. I like dares because I refuse to lose a dare. Taking up the sword, I tore down the fortress, exposing the secrets they contained behind the walls. The company didn't go broke, we didn't lose money, and we continued to pull together to make technology work while they were replaced. While it is an inconvenience, it is not a death sentence to replace your IT staff.

> **The human face is a mirror to the soul and will reveal true feelings.**

Finding the right technical people is challenging but doable. I used to love the old *Saturday Night Live* skits with Jimmy Fallon as Nick Burns, the computer guy. Nick would be called in to fix the employees' computers. He would use jargon they couldn't understand, act like they were stupid, and finally tell them, "Move," so he could sit down to fix the issue in one keystroke. Then he would get out of their chair, acting like a jerk and calling them idiots.

As part of our IT hiring process now, we not only look for someone with the technical skills and educational background, but we examine his or her face. Facial expressions can tell you a great deal about the person you are hiring. The human face is a mirror to the soul and will reveal true feelings.

Our most successful programmer sits behind a computer screen filled with gobbledygook in a dark room, but when we walk down the hallway to say good morning, his face lights up with a genuine smile. He makes that same expression when we ask him to write in new code. At his interview, his genuine smile let us know we had the right guy for the job. His standard answer for any request is, "Sure! Oh, sure I can do that. When do you need this done by?"

Part of hiring a great techie is to ask about his or her

problem-solving skills to eliminate typical mistakes and reduce the number of questions staff might have daily. By adding a self-help virtual robot to our computer system that any employee can access at any time, we have cut the number of computer issues down by 80 percent. This has only been achieved by keeping track of common problems and developing a step-by-step instructional for each.

With the use of a simple cell phone camera, it is easy to take a picture or video tutorial to walk employees through easy fixes that take less time for them to do themselves versus calling IT to do it.

With 200 employees, we staff two programmers. Having a programmer has allowed the company to expand our CARS system to include automating our billing system, payroll, and an early warning system for potential client problems.

In addition to the programmers, the company staffs two problem ticket IT people who also develop the training bots and add to the catalog as they find answers to the problem tickets. Our staff has coverage 24x7. That means that the company is making money 24x7 and our generators never go down.

Another function of our technical department is creating a company newsletter. They are responsible for gathering content, such as adding the latest innovations and how to find faster resolutions to common problems. Plus, the department confers with Human Resources to throw in birthdays and anniversary dates. The lights in their department are usually out to protect their eyes, but their sense of humor is very illuminating. Often the newsletters have at least one film clip to lighten the whole company mood.

Since these tech-savvy people have access to client email addresses, it becomes easy for them to send out bulk emails to clients, and post content to manage social accounts. They can't do this without your participation. You, as the owner, have to direct what content is going to be pushed out. What you say to your clients and staff must have meaning. No one wants to read blah-blah; customers desire information that they can use. Feed them a monthly snippet that is short, concise, and that they can use to improve their partnership with you.

Moses would have used his IT department to communicate with all his people wandering in the desert. He wouldn't have needed as many managers per person. Can you imagine the organization he could have assembled with a programmer? Your company doesn't have to wander aimlessly when you employ and use your technical people fearlessly.

. . . . . . . . . . . . . . . . . . . . . . . . . . . . . . . . . . . . . . . . . . .

**Lesson Learned:** The pit crew uses power tools and technology to quickly put the driver back on the track to win the race.

# CHAPTER 27

# Dirty Rotten Scoundrels

> *"Remember that naughty kid in high school who was likable, funny, and a scoundrel? Some grow up and become dirty rotten scoundrels."*

Some people are so fearful of being cheated that it paralyzes them in business. Here is a fact—someone along the way will steal from you or cheat or lie. It is one of the reasons that the term "buckle up" is so important. When theft and cheating occur, the situation jolts you. If you are buckled in, then you know what could happen and have taken precautions to stay firmly seated. The seatbelt is proven to save a life; that is why there is a law mandating that you wear one. The police department knows that there is always a risk of an accident. The collision may not be your fault, but crashes happen in life.

> **If you venture out into your own retail business, then you will encounter a shoplifter.**

Besides the ultimate theft of our company, there are many other instances of dirty rotten scoundrels throughout the years. It happens to everyone at least once.

Jerry, one of the programmers that worked on our beloved CARS software, became disgruntled and fantasized that CARS was suffering due to lack of care. The computer program was, after all, a living entity that only he could adequately nurture. Jerry offloaded the program and took it away so he could raise the android properly. The police came for Jerry. Then Jerry sued the company. Jerry is now $25,000 richer because it was more expensive to hire a lawyer than to pay Jerry to go away. Talk about leaving a sour taste in your mouth; this situation still makes my blood boil to think about.

If you venture out into your own retail business, then you will encounter a shoplifter. No matter how many sensors, beepers, or cameras you use, there is a creative thief out there that thought of something you haven't. The fact that theft is going to happen doesn't mean you should not try everything you can to prevent it, because you have to work. What I am saying is, "Don't be surprised when something disappears."

The ultimate scoundrel is the employee that steals, lies, or cheats. Yes, those church people you hired will cheat, too. That is why Jesus said, "None of you are without sin." They went to church and confessed, but they still took your money. Now, most likely, the church people will be the honest ones, but I'm just saying, don't be surprised when it happens.

The next unscrupulous bunch of scoundrels might be the clients. Everyone wants something for nothing. Whatever you are charging, your client probably thinks it is too much. We have had clients go bankrupt and leave us holding the bag on their bill way too many times to write about in this book. There is usually a pattern where you can see that they are having financial difficulty, but you want to think the best of people. In a service-based business, you have delivered service and expect payment once the job is done. In a retail business, you have some control in that you can withhold product until payment.

Heck, even your friends will cheat you, or should I say *especially* your friends will cheat you?

We shared space at a yearly convention with a dear friend, Leroy. I had always loved Leroy! He is funny, talks up a good story, and being with him feels like family. The agreement was easy: half and half. A handshake and a laugh sealed the deal.

The first year we paid the bill for the space and sent

Leroy an invoice that was promptly paid. The second year we did the same, but Leroy didn't pay. With the third year approaching, our friend firmly apologized for the over sight and said he would pay both invoices as soon as we could send them. "Make sure you send last year's invoice and this year together."

Guess what: Leroy still hasn't paid. He is having financial problems within his company.

You can be overly paranoid to the point that you lose track of the business at hand. Even the shrewdest among us get scammed, lied to, and taken advantage of at times. The very fact that you are creating a business makes you vulnerable to predators and shady characters. The perception is that you are rich because you own a business. You know that isn't the truth, especially after reading this book! However, perception is the reality, so if you have money, then others think you can afford to give it to them. In fact, many people believe because you have money, you *should* give it to them!

> **If they talk about how it was always someone else's fault, then it will be your fault when they fail.**

One way to protect your business is to confirm a conversation or agreement—either informally via email or formally with a contract. I have failed to do this on several occasions. Either I got busy and forgot or didn't think it was necessary. Sometimes it worked out fine; other times, I had a loss. I have learned over the years to stop what I am doing to email (document) the conversation so that we all are on the same page.

Watch and listen to how your potential business partner, clients, or prospective employees talk about and deal with other people. Their behavior will give you a pretty accurate clue as to how they'll treat you. If they talk about how it was always someone else's fault, then it will be your fault when they fail.

The good news is that most people are honest and mean well. The bad guys or girls aren't the rule, but there are enough of them around to make life interesting.

Encourage all employees who handle accounting and payment functions to take vacation time, with another person handling their work in their absence. This fresh set of eyes may detect questionable practices or trends. I call this discovery. We have a team that covers vacations. Our coverage team as been valuable in that they have found training issues, holes in an employee's education, or laziness that needed to be corrected. We have learned over the years when an employee doesn't want his or her work covered, there is usually an underlying problem that they don't want others to discover.

Check your bank statements. Even though accounting might be over your head, tracking the incoming and outgoing money will give you a view of your cash. I print the report out so I can highlight questions to quiz our accountant. The simple step of inquiring can alert your accounting staff that you are watching and your eyes are open.

Our office manager decided to condense the credit card statements for each of our managers onto a spreadsheet. She thought this would help me see the categories of expenditures easily. Her columns showed totals for lodging, meals, etc., as a total. The problem with this was that she was the one determining what column the charge should sit, and she was the only one looking at the expense and amount. I explained to her that I appreciated her forethought, but I still wanted to put my eyes on the actual statement to prevent theft.

Once your enterprise has positive cash flow, you will be able to set aside a small percentage of profit for write-offs. A small amount in a separate savings of even 0.01 percent can keep you from worrying over lost revenue. At the end of the year, the savings will either go to losses or be the spare change in your pocket.

. . . . . . . . . . . . . . . . . . . . . . . . . . . . . . . . . . . . . . . . .

**Lesson Learned:** Race car drivers know that something is going to break on the car and they are going to have to pay to fix it.

# CHAPTER 28

# Hatchet Man

*"Who ya gonna call When the employment hatchet needs to fall?"*

— *Hatchet Man*

I hate firing people. It sucks. I feel like I am ruining their lives, so early in the company, I would wait to see if they would quit on their own. I learned some insightful information along the way that has changed my viewpoint on terminating employment.

In the beginning of our business, when we had a smaller office, we all worked close to each other. The office was a big open space with our desks end-to-end so we could work as a team to complete the work. The staff was mostly women in an enclosed area, and it was critical that we all get along. For the most part, we shared similar views, and getting along well worked up until the day that Julie came into the office.

Julie was a complainer. She didn't show up on time, and she was not a team player. Julie needed to go, but none of us wanted to fire her because of her nasty nature. Our team of women was anxious and nervous about dealing with ugly-acting people. None of us liked harsh confrontations. So Rich was officially deemed the hatchet man.

We were very specific with his instructions. "Make Julie get her stuff before you fire her because we don't want to see her after you do. Do not let her back into the office."

Hatchet Man asked Julie to come into the kitchen. "Julie, can you step over to the kitchen for a minute? Oh, when you come, bring your purse."

> **It isn't fair to the high-functioning employees to see that the company is retaining an employee with poor performance. When the boss doesn't have enough guts to address issues, the company loses credibility.**

Julie was never to be seen again, and from that day forward when Rich asked to talk to anyone, they would always ask, "Do I need to bring my purse?" This statement has been somewhat of a running joke for the last 20 years. However, in some cases, it is a cloud that hangs over the company. We have not always dealt with employees fairly.

What is fair?

First of all, it isn't fair to the high-functioning employees to see that the company is retaining an employee with poor performance. Also, believe me—the employees are noticing who shows up late, and who has the Monday flu. When the boss doesn't have enough guts to address these issues, then the company loses credibility.

Next, it isn't fair to the under-performing employees to be kept employed. They are underperforming for a reason. They either don't like the job, they don't like the company, or employees are not wired to do what they are doing. Remember the birds and fish story? By keeping these underachieving employees, you are preventing them from moving to a career that they enjoy. You are delaying their train to happiness.

An excellent example of this was poor Helen. She was the sweetest lady, and her job was to pick up documents and deliver them to different dealerships. Helen squeaked a bit when she talked, and her voice projected a nasal quality. Poor Helen could not make the drive from the dealership to dealership without getting lost, no matter how precise the navigational instructions. This wandering resulted in scolding Helen on most days. She would smile during the discipline and apologize, "I know. I get so turned around sometimes. I will highlight the map tomorrow. I know that I can follow the roads that way."

The delay in scheduling meant that every employee would now be behind in their work. Now they would be late going home, plus having to be unproductive while waiting for Helen. The lack of productivity affected their paycheck, which in turn affected their feelings toward Helen.

By the time Hatchet Man Rich got around to firing her, Helen was so relieved that she hugged him. Little did we know that she hadn't been able to muster up the nerve to quit and needed Rich to give her that kick in the butt to move onto her next job.

> **In most cases you will pay unemployment, so get over the sting of the ruling and move on with business.**

Up until I understood these principles, I always thought that Rich was unfeeling and callous. I used to ask him what he said to people when he let them go. He answered with a serious face, "I told them they can work anywhere they want to, but just not here." Obviously, that isn't true, or poor Helen wouldn't have hugged him.

Rich's hard reality is the more compassionate response to discontinuing employment. A lesson we can all remember.

Let's take a moment to speak of unemployment. Yes, you will most likely pay the government the money to pay your ex-employee. We have been in the situation more than once where the employee failed to show up for days on end with no phone call, no email, nothing to indicate that they were alive, sick, or had quit. We have a statement in our human resources manual documenting the following: *When failing to call, email, text, or notify the company of absence within 24 hours of not attending work, we assume the employee has resigned.* Even with this statement, the unemployment office has sided with the employee for benefits. What I am saying is, that in most cases you will pay, so get over the sting of the ruling and move on with business. Don't stay stuck on the pain or you will be losing more money worrying about lost cash.

Here are some DOs that can help.

> *After every conversation, email the employee the discussion and the results.*
>
> *Specify the expectations for the future in the email.*
>
> *When an employee doesn't show up for work, call and leave a message; record the call if you can.*
>
> *Email the employee after the call to document that you left a message.*

If the employee is a no-show, include the phrase, "Upon no communication within 24 hours, the company will assume this is your resignation."

The above sounds easy-peasy, but the fact is that taking a moment to carry through with the steps is very difficult. Life happens, calls come in, other employees need your help, and before you know what hit you, documenting the situation gets forgotten. I have now found it helpful to write a sticky note, "email Jane Doe's failure to appear and the time" and stick it on my computer. This way, I don't forget and can go back to the task later.

**Lesson Learned:** A race car driver doesn't keep the guy that forgot to tighten his lug nuts.

# CHAPTER 29

# Geez, Don't Get Defensive

*"When you get defensive, you skip the valuable lesson that could benefit your business."*

I was once hired by a fixed operations manager to go to all the dealerships in his zone to train his service staff on warranty policy. I enjoy training because it allows me to help people understand the process and make their jobs easier. It was a good gig because I could visit four dealerships a week in the area and split the travel charges between the dealerships, saving their company money and our time by condensing travel hours.

The fixed operations manager is the liaison between the service managers of each individual dealership and the corporate company. However, each dealership has a general manager who is responsible for his or her own store. This person is the decision maker for the corporate company in that store, and answers for the dealership he or she oversees. The general manager approves expenditures for his or her own dealership.

I wrongly assumed that the general manager of each store knew that I was in his service department training his staff. That only stood to reason that I would be presenting my bill to the office manager when the training was complete. I blindly thought that the fixed operations manager had informed the general manager for each location.

General Managers have a somewhat intimidating persona. They usually have a large, ornate office, giving them an aura of power. Mike fit this description. He also had a reputation for being a hot-head—a volcano that often erupted. Mike's impeccable suit fit over a muscular body of power ending in manicured nails. Smiling wasn't a quality that came naturally; most often, his mouth showed the clench of teeth hidden behind his lips. He was an immaculate dictator of a small kingdom. Mike started each day marching through the departments, nodding at the managers, illuminating his presence on the premises. The department heads notified staff that the ruler was in for the day and that all systems needed to run full power.

It's no wonder that my armpits had pearls of sweat

dripping from them when he called me to his office during my training at his dealership.

As soon as the door closed behind me, the lava started spewing from his lips. He began his tirade: "What makes you think you can come into my dealership without contacting me first? I have an invoice from your company in my hand that I did not agree to in any form. This is my dealership. I approve who performs work in any capacity inside these walls. The fixed operations manager does not pay my bills. He has no signing power or access to my checkbook. How do you intend to be paid for this training?"

Well, crap! He was mad but as scary as he was, he was right. The final payment would have his signature on any check issued at that dealership. I had missed the mark because I didn't even think about notifying him of my trip. Heck, I didn't introduce myself at all during the training of his people.

I held my head up and looked directly into his fire-lit brown eyeballs. "You're right. You were completely bypassed."

> **If you use "but"—then you are a butt.**

Silence hit the office, and the heat that Mike radiated cooled from 200 degrees Fahrenheit down to 80 degrees.

I continued after a moment of thought, "I should not have assumed the fixed operations manager had informed you. You have the wallet for the store, and you are the one that has to pay. I totally missed the boat on this. I tell you what, let's ignore that invoice and start this relationship all over again, this time respectful of your position."

In that moment of silence, I noticed the pictures of his family on his credenza. They sparked one more comment from me. "In looking at that picture of your kids, it reminds me of all the times that my kids assumed that their dad told me where they were going. Dad got busy and forgot to tell me. When I arrived home, and the kids were missing, I was clueless to where they were, what they were doing, and thinking the worst, I thought they were missing."

Mike's furnace continued to cool while his body relaxed under the grey fitted jacket. His knees bent slightly as he unplanted his stance from a firm pole to the military at ease. He responded almost humbly, "Let's take a second and sit down. I don't want you to write off the invoice just yet. Tell me what you are offering and then we can see if there can be an agreed price if I like the value."

Mike ended up being an excellent friend after this and purchased training several more times for his dealership.

Notice one thing that never happened in this confrontation: the word "but" was never uttered. Had I used that word, Mike's heater would have never cooled down. Let's look at how this could have ended differently.

Notice I said, "I should not have assumed the fixed

operations manager had informed you." Not, "But I assumed the fixed operation manager informed you."

There is no "but" because I am responsible as a business owner to cover my bases. If I had used the "but" phrase, the outcome would have been totally different.

"But" is an out that lets you not take responsibility.

"But" is a defensive move that you think takes the blame off you and assigns blame on what comes after the "but."

If you use "but"—then you are a butt.

---

**Lesson Learned:** You have never heard a race car driver say, "I could have won that race, but the crew was slow replacing the tire."

# CHAPTER 30

# Succession—Ugh, I Never Want to Leave

> *"Train up a child in the way he should go, And when he is old he will not depart from it."*
>
> *— Proverbs 22:6*
> *New King James Version*
> *(NKJV)*

Quicker than I could blink, my 66th birthday arrived. Just like every other old fart, I feel 35 inside, and all is well until the mirror says, "Hold on there, you ain't no spring chick, girl."

I have witnessed many companies where the owners held on too long, only to see their baby start to fail. Sometimes the owners should have celebrated by leaving while they were at the top of their game. Remember back to the chapter where I talked about moving up and out of my roles as administrator and manager? What are you going to do if you don't work in the business every day?

Not only might it be time to let go of the day-to-day process so you can enjoy a bit of life, but there may also be a need for loosening the reins.

Time is a commodity that we can never get back, and you spent enormous amounts on your child—the business. We talked about the infant years, toddler phase, teen years, and here we are—your business is all grown up. If you raised the company the way it should go, you can take time to go forward and enjoy the years and travel with all the other old farts.

> **If you raised the company the way it should go, you can take time now for yourself.**

For you, this phase may be your time to relax on the beach, golf, be with family or do any number of things that you have been dying to do (no pun there—but you do want to enjoy life before you go!). I mean, you don't want employees to find you at your final resting place at your desk one of these days.

As for the need to give some slack in the reins, a few relevant reasons might be:

> *You want new and fresh ideas coming into the business for it to keep growing and stay current with the industry.*
>
> *Modern technology is emerging and beyond your scope to adapt.*
>
> *Relationships change and younger mentality is on the rise in your industry.*
>
> *Energy is low, and sales are stagnating.*
>
> *Goodness, maybe you're getting a little more tired!*

Perhaps you are selling the company and cashing in on the sale will give you money for the rest of your life. We are selling to David. I know you may think, "Why would you make your own son buy the company he worked so hard to build?" The answer is simple; he needs skin in the game. Yes, David has put much sweat into the corporation and revolutionized systems. Being an owner is far different because the successes, failures, employees, and profitability are on your shoulders. Moreover, Mama needs the money!

Preparing for succession is hard, takes some planning, and hurts as you loosen the reins.

### *Step 1: Look at your foundation and the values that created the company*

It is vital that the core values stay intact as new ideas come in. The entire foundation block in our company is the highest standard for ethics. The mission statement and values don't change, but the methods to get there change drastically.

Our core statement is: *Do the right thing every time, especially when it is hard.* That is a constant and static belief.

Every department must add to the bricks on this foundation. You might redecorate the house. Heck, you will even tear down walls, and for sure you are going to put in new bathroom plumbing and fixtures. You will not be digging up the foundation to update a home. Those cornerstones are the most critical piece of your business as well.

> **The mission statement and values don't change, but the methods change drastically.**

When planning succession or sale of the business, the foundation will go with the people, family, or new company buying or inheriting it. As you step back into a lesser role in the daily operation, you will have trained your managers and staff to continue to live with your values.

Often, Rich has had to scrape me off the wall to make me do the right thing. I can't tell you how many times I have been tempted to cheat just a wee bit, believing perhaps no one would find out. That little devil sits on my left shoulder and shouts in my ear, "Hey, it is no big deal! Change the date and bring that dollar figure to the acceptable range in your favor! Yes, go right ahead and make life better for yourself! It's easy!"

My angel, in the form of Rich, my recovering alcoholic husband, sits in front of me and can see that little devil nagging me to cheat. He reminds me of the firm cement of the company, founded on doing the right thing. I cave in and flick Satan from my shoulder while anger rises in my body because I know that doing the right thing is going to cost me money. Most choices will come down to that—money. That was why I was tempted to do the wrong thing. Yes, the almighty dollar will lead you astray.

David has witnessed that struggle and knows the proper answer to the integrity dilemma. He is trained the way he should go and will not stray from honesty no matter the cost.

You, the creator, owner, and commander-in-chief, may need to stay as part of the foundation for several years before you can exit the company entirely. Even though, toward the end of the transition, you might not feel like you are doing much, you are keeping the bottom mortar of the company intact.

These last years are ones filled with talking. You will start to see yourself as a counselor, so you might as well install a couch for people to lie on and tell you their problems. Staff, managers, and executive teams will be in, asking questions and just talking to get your view on issues and changes. It feels like all you do is chat all day long, and that chatting is what you should be doing.

### *Step 2: Put the executive team in place*

The executive team members are the people that have been with you several years and have proven their skills and loyalty. Whether you are selling the business or grooming family for ownership, you will need an executive team for the next several years to guide the way.

> **Just like breathing, old air must go out before you take in a new breath.**

These are the people that know the core values, the mission, the clients, and the staff well. Those tough individuals that make hard choices and decisions daily probably will be part of the sale or transition. They will guide the next owners in the business. Sometimes they will not be staying on with the new owners, but most of the time they are needed to show the ropes and remove any obstacles to the transition.

Much like an engineer knows which walls cannot be torn down because they are load bearing, these people know the absolutes that will never change.

### *Step 3: Don't freak out*

You have figuratively lived in this home all your life, the company home. It is natural that the wallpaper you love will be pulled down by the new owners. The fact is, it is probably old, ugly, and needs a facelift. Don't freak out because of the changes you see happening around you. Just like breathing, old air must go out before you take in a new breath. As long as they don't mess with the foundation, the business will adapt to new methods.

Our son, David, is our successor. He has been in training since he was little. He started from the ground up and spent many years learning each job in the business. Even at six years old, he could staple papers for us on the right corner only. However, more than the training, he has the temperament for ownership. He ponders problems without making knee-jerk reactions. We have watched him make changes to each department after careful consideration and given him the freedom to make a mistake now and again.

Part of his wiring is to procrastinate, which will not work in the company's best interest. We could talk 'til we were blue in the face about getting projects completed in a timely way. No words could make him change. It was only after failing because of his lack of urgency that he realized giving into his desire not to handle things promptly would eventually cause him to fail.

### *Finally—Find your next passion*

Although your job may never terminate entirely, your hands-on time in the business will dwindle, leaving you feeling unneeded or underused. You are still on-call for managers as they acclimate to the job of being in charge. Financial matters, forecasting, profitability, insurance, taxes, loans, and other issues will need your attention. All of this isn't the same as being in the trenches with the troops.

> **Don't let the employees find you dead in your chair—go forth—forge a new frontier.**

At this point, I found myself wandering into the office daily with a sense of loss. I heard the stillness where there was once a buzzing of energy. Sadness covered my face as I sat in my beautiful, lonely office, and I only brightened when one of the crew would wander in to ask for information or help. My email box was clean, and I organized files on my computer with a vengeance. I cleaned every desk drawer and revamped to *Better Homes &Gardens* standards.

The lowest point of my life came as I realized I am

surely going to die because I have lost one of the biggest loves of my life. Tears flowed in sorrow.

That is when the determined young girl inside screamed at the top of her lungs, "You stupid idiot! Get your rear in gear and live to your next potential."

There is nothing quite like kicking your own self in the ass.

There might be a passion that you ignored that you will be able to pursue. Now is the time you can commit to helping a charity, do some writing, get involved volunteering, or start another business. I chose to do all of the above but this time, I have created a smaller company that is a less complicated monster to corral.

I am pursuing my passion, which is writing. I probably will never be on the *New York Times* bestseller list, but I am writing about what is close to my heart. I have five children's books published, and three of the five have won prestigious awards! *Football Flyboy* is a memoir about my Dad during WWII and flying around the world. (Wow, can I put in a note here? That was rewarding.) The audio book received the honor of a gold medal at the Benjamin Franklin awards. Starting this new path has enriched my mind and given me renewed youth and energy to learn something new every day.

Charities are another passion that I am blessed to participate whole-heartedly in now. The new business is in property rentals with a responsible manager in place and static income. Having a manager that I trained well means that I don't have to worry about the problems on site.

I am meeting new people in new industries. Opening my mind, I am getting a little more liberal, which has Rich calling me a left-wing democrat. I keep telling him that I am a moderate.

Don't let the employees find you dead in your chair—go forth—forge a new frontier.

**Lesson Learned:** Drivers retire from the track, but never from racing.

# CHAPTER 31

# The Halfway Point is Not the End

*"If I've learned anything, it is that the halfway point is age 92 because I am going to keep going with new adventures, enriching my mind, and living to the fullest."*

— Lisa Reinicke

The halfway point only marks the end of the beginning. This point is where I choose to leave the story. When you get to the end of the race, there is always another race. There may be a race with a bigger team or a longer track, depending on your choices.

Your book of life is a series of chapters to write, and the next chapter is waiting for you to pen. Whether you are just starting in business, thinking about owning a business, or at the end of the racetrack, one thing is for sure—being in business for yourself is a wild ride. Just as race car driving isn't like normal driving—on the track, everything is amplified. That race car will toss you about, yank you to and fro, and as the checkered flag is waved, you will feel exhausted. However, racing is an adrenaline rush like no other.

> **The chapters of our lives together come together to make a story of grace.**

I think back to everything my Dad taught me growing up and how it applies to business. Dad was right; all things work out over time. The lessons he taught me paid off in life.

> *Your authentic self needs to show up every day.*
> *Work hard, not just hard, but really hard.*
> *The school of hard knocks is an actual school, so go to school every day and learn something.*
> *Stop whining.*
> *You're going to be OK.*
> *What's done is done; get over it.*

I found that my blessings are things I didn't see along the way. They are things I certainly didn't deserve. Looking back, I see the breadcrumbs of blessings in my path. My destiny was just like Ruth in the Bible when the workers were instructed to purposely drop leftover wheat in the fields so Ruth could feed her family. In retrospect, God intervened for me every step of the way.

Life has given Rich and me an education beyond a doctorate. Our marriage is unbelievably soul-melded as we continue to weather storms, sunshine, rain, and on into autumn with beautiful harmony. The chapters of our lives together come together to make a story of grace.

If I can do this, you can, too. Living is about doing; not merely trying. We all must keep driving after the checkered flag to finish the race.

The book of your life includes many casts of characters. You interact with them, change them, and love them. These characters are there to change the leading player, and the main character is there to change them. A dance—a complicated, beautiful, challenging dance—is worth the energy. Having your own business is a huge undertaking and an enormous reward to the group on the dance floor.

Don't give up. Don't give in. Hold fast to what you believe in doing. When you're down, you're not out. When you're poor, that is what will make you rich. Mistakes will make you grow. Sorrows will make you appreciate joy. Yin and yang go together.

When you feel like you will never make it, remember my

story. I was a little orphan, adopted by great parents. I was a nobody. I didn't have a great education. I had hardships. You will have difficulties too. You have your own suitcase of problems; keep unpacking until you solve them.

In my teen years, my Dad took me to the demolition derby. Old cars with souped-up engines would race in a figure-eight track. As they would enter the intersection of the figure-eight, one after another, the vehicles crashed, taking each other out of the race. The last car running was the winner.

He was excited as he called out the racers, "Watch, Lisa. Watch. Ohhh No! Now this guy coming into the turn, watch him let off the gas just before he goes into the intersection. He is staging himself not to be hit."

> **Know when to speed up, slow down, and brake; watch the corners; stay clear of damage; and stay on the track.**

The fewer drivers that remained, the more commentary came from Dad, "Number five there. This guy is smart. He knows when to brake to avoid a collision. Lisa, knowing when to speed up and slow down, that is what wins the race. Oh, and look. Number five, he is watching for the right opportunity to enter that X."

I never realized that what Dad taught me about the demolition derby actually prepared me for business. The lesson must have resided in my subconscious all these years.

Know when to speed up, slow down, and brake; watch the corners; stay clear of damage; and stay on the track.

**Lesson Learned:** Race car drivers don't let the fear of crashing keep them from driving.

# Epilogue

I hope you enjoyed the true stories in this book. With constant information overload, we get bombarded with daily, useful information can be forgotten.

Stories help jog the memory and give the brain something to relate to in times of need.

The information in this book can be a reference tool that you can look back on as your company grows. Whether you are a small shop or working toward substantial growth, there are a few nuggets buried in the book for you to dig out.

Writing this book was a personal look at my life, challenges, hopes, dreams, failures, and successes. Some were hard to expose and came with the fear of judgment. In the end, I wanted the reader to know that even the people who look like they "have it all" have grave problems. However, I also wanted you to know there is hope for success.

Every person pays the price for choices made in his or her life. There were choices that I spent a high dollar for in relationships. Much work went into correcting failures and setbacks.

If I were unwilling to expose my raw self, then the reader would not see the full impact of the toll on the life choice of owning a business.

The choice to work for yourself is not as tricky as choosing for others to work with you. They both still impact your family and company. Having accomplished the goal, I can say the payment was worth the struggles.

Our company has benefited thousands of lives and provided a living for hundreds of families. Passing the baton to a new generation, I know that the dream will go on. More people will be blessed.

> *"It is well, it is well with my soul."*
> — Horatio Spafford

# Authors Note

The first step is always the hardest, except for that second step. The third step isn't much easier. Pretty soon though you learn to run, and then you fall down because you ran too fast. You can pretty much count on getting hurt by running or falling down sometimes. The chances are that you will bump into other people along the way. They might skin their knee too when you unintentionally knock them off balance.

Don't lose your honest self in the process of ownership. No matter how hard life gets, or how short you are on time, take precious seconds to be kind even when you are taking a firm stance.

Set boundaries and live within them. Make sure others know where the in-field is. Set new boundaries as you grow.

Remember that if a little girl with no formal education can succeed, then you can too.

Put your helmet on, buckle your seatbelt, and get your business going.

# Acknowledgements

I wrote this book to give others inspiration to live their own dream; being in business for yourself. There is a big difference between just opening a business and developing that vision into a company.

Life has a way of getting in the way. I hope my story can fill the reader with enough determination to experience the wild ride of success.

Thank you to my children. You ate dinner on my papers while I worked. Then splashed bathwater on important documents because the only time left to work at night was while you were soaking. You all have turned into magnificent people. That is the best success anyone can have as a parent.

Thanks to Rich, my poor husband, who agreed to expose our baggage so that the reader could have the true transparent story that tells the sacrifice of success.

For the over 200 of the most amazing talented people; you are the backbone that makes our invention work.

A big thanks to Alexandra O'Connell for pulling the

details out of me and organizing thoughts and edits. And Kathy Meis at Bublish for all the fine tuning, layout, cover design, and just plain putting up with me to get this book done. I can't leave out Shilah at Bublish for taking every phone call and email to accomplish this story. I might add that these ladies joyfully took calls at all hours without complaining. Big hug and praise to Kayla my publicist for all the hours put into selling my books to those near and far. Plus organizing every event and my life.

# About the Author

Lisa Reinicke is the founder and CEO of Automotive Warranty Network, a company with over 200 employees helping more than 800 dealerships nationwide. Her mission with AWN is to provide quality service to their clients while offering a decent living and balanced lifestyle to the employees by adding continuous training and education programs. She is also the majority owner of Our House Properties and owns and manages multiple mountain properties.

She is the majority holder of Our House Publications and author of five published children's picture books and other non-fiction books. Lisa was honored with the *Mom's Choice Gold Award* for lifetime literary excellence for her children's book *Wings and Feet* in 2017 and *Wilhelmina's Wish* in 2019. Her other children's books carry *Book Excellence* and *Purple Dragonfly* winners. *Football Flyboy*, a memoir about a cocky WW2 pilot was awarded the *Benjamin Franklin Award* in 2019. Lisa passionately works raising money for charities that improve children's lives physically, emotionally, and spiritually. She serves on several boards of directors for companies helping to direct cash flow and maintain company policy and high standards. Connect with her socially through the channels below.

Website LisaReinicke.com https://www.lisareinicke.com/

Facebook https://www.facebook.com/lisareinicke

Twitter https://twitter.com/lisaauthor

Instagram https://www.instagram.com/lisareinicke_author

YouTube https://www.youtube.com/channel/UCjPwSKkA0ox7dmBf7EqJ6FQ

Amazon https://www.amazon.com/-/e/B01N0T838X

**Also by Lisa Reinicke**

Arnold the Cute Little Pig with Personality
Bart's Escape Out the Gate
Wings and Feet
Wilhelmina's Wish
David's Christmas Wish
Football Flyboy
Toast with a Side of Dragon
How to Write a Children's Picture Book

www.ingramcontent.com/pod-product-compliance
Lightning Source LLC
Chambersburg PA
CBHW070732020526
44118CB00035B/1214